WATER
BY THE
INCH

Francis Asbury Young and Eva Naomi Lawrence Young, circa 1882

WATER BY THE INCH

Adventures of a Pioneer Family
on an Arizona Desert Homestead

BY HERBERT V. YOUNG

Northland Press — Flagstaff, Arizona

To my father and my mother,
whose love, care, and teaching did so much
to shape the lives of their children,
this book is dedicated in loving memory.

CONTENTS

Prologue

"DAD, WHY DON'T YOU GIVE OTHERS A CHANCE TO READ of your adventures on a desert homestead in your younger years?" my son Bert asked. "You aren't too old to write another book."

"Better get with it, Gramps," Bert's son, Bud, cut in. "Tell how you were washed down the Agua Fria River after a cloudburst . . ."

"And got trapped in a den of gila monsters . . ." added Bert's second son, Ken.

"And how a bird saved your life," contributed my daughter Gerry.

"Those stories would make good reading," Bert agreed, "but even more human interest would lie in the record of a pioneer family's struggle to hack a living out of a piece of virgin desert. The way you've told it to us, there must have been an awful lot of hard work and disappointment."

"But compensation, too," I said. "Even in the most primitive conditions there can be a lot of happiness in a home."

With my wife, "Zip," joining the urging, I agreed to have at it.

Eighty years have passed since the occurrence of the last events recalled here. Yet my memory of most of those things in which I was a figure is keen. This is due to the fact that my father's homestead was

1

located on the fringe of the inhabited area of Arizona's Salt River Valley, with primitive desert on all four sides. Thus, we were far from clamors and pressures of the city, enabling my impressions to be implanted so deeply that I have found little difficulty in bringing them to life. I have been aided by the recollections of my brother and sisters, and the stories told by my mother in the later years of her life, also by old letters found in my mother's trunk, and letters my father wrote to a brother detailing some of his experiences after his arrival.

The people the reader will encounter in these pages are either real or true to types I have known. I have presented a description of things as they existed in one section of Arizona in the last two decades of the nineteenth century. Where advisable, I have used fictitious names.

From the time I could walk, I loved the desert and found pleasure in wandering among its trees and flowers, finding something new in desert life on every trip. I disagree with those who assert that to be found there are only those things that sting, stab, strike, or stink, obviously referring to scorpions, cactus, rattlesnakes, and skunks. I have found them to be more interesting than dangerous. In my memory, the pleasant things are the outstanding ones—the balmy springs with their carpets of flowers and enticing odors, the trees blazing with golden bloom, the fascinating wild life, and, during the hot but bearable summers, sleeping outdoors with the stars shining brilliantly through air untainted by dust or smoke. Autumns were pleasant, winters, mild. I spent the first eleven years of my life on that ranch my father carved out of the Arizona desert. It lay fifteen miles from Phoenix, which was little more than a village when my father arrived in Arizona. It is now one of the most populous areas of the Southwest.

Before undertaking my writing job, I decided I should revisit our old ranchsite. With my daughter driving, we traveled south from our home in the beautiful Verde Valley to Phoenix. For most of the hundred mile trip we rode on a divided speedway, often noting lateral scars on nearby mountainsides that marked the course of the old stage and wagon road from Phoenix to points north. On that same road ninety years before, my father and mother had traveled in a covered wagon from desert heat to cool pine country, and I had crossed it in a primitive automobile thirty years later.

We came out of the mountains through low hills to the level floor of the valley. Though still twenty-five miles from the heart of the city, we saw buildings everywhere. There were housing developments, commercial structures, a race track with stables, an electronics factory, and a large shopping center with nationally known names displayed on fine buildings.

Already we were well within the area called by its citizens metropolitan Phoenix, which includes several other interlocking municipalities. The population is well over a million persons, and it spreads over an area of several hundred square miles.

A haze carrying the odor of exhaust fumes hung over the city, almost obscuring the surrounding mountains. Through this haze a number of high-rise buildings thrust their towering pillars of steel, brick, tile, and glass toward a sky that not so long ago had been crystal clear and occupied only by birds in flight.

Passing through twenty miles of buildings erected on land that had once seen only saguaros, cholla, palo verde, and other forms of desert life, we came to Camelback Road, named for the mountain that is Phoenix's most famous landmark; this thoroughfare led directly to the land on which I had first seen light. Many times in my young life I had traveled this road behind a team of horses moving between irrigated fields; then, the surface might be either heavy dust or mud as the weather decreed. Now, business buildings lined the paved street for miles.

Toward the end of the trip we came to some open fields, planted to alfalfa and root crops. A few white-faced cattle grazed in fenced areas, their blocky bodies greatly different from the rangy descendents of Texas longhorns with which I had been so familiar in my younger days. Only a couple of miles from the land my father homesteaded was a supermarket, and though not visible, we knew that not far to the south was one of the valley's many golf courses.

I knew the old homesite was at the intersection of Camelback Road and 107th Avenue. Reaching that spot, I found nothing at all to remind me of the place where I had been born. A house sat where my father's apiary once had been, in the southeast corner of the tract, but all the rest was in crops.

We drove north a mile. All land had been cleared. Not far to the east was the spot where I had located the flowering desert lily, Queen of the Night. A big machine was harvesting carrots there, spilling them into a dump truck. Not a cactus, not a mesquite, not a wildflower was in sight—just croplands stretching endlessly. Where the canals could not supply water, wells had been drilled, extending the croplands even further into the desert. Fortunately for those who love the desert as it was created, there are still many areas in the Southwest with their natural beauties intact, safe from settlement and vandals alike. I visited some of these spots in refreshing my memory of the events I have recorded here. It has been pleasant to view again the desert colors—the olive and gray-greens of greasewood and sage, the ochre and tan of the desert floor—and the distant blue and purple mountains seen through crystal clear air, and to savor once more the delightful perfumes so distinctive of the wild lands.

CHAPTER 1

"Geronimo Is Out There"

1886

MY FATHER SMELLED POWDER SMOKE WITHIN THIRTY MIN-utes after he left the train at Benson. It can well be said that Arizona received him with a bang.

Following the example of ancestors who had been moving west-ward for more than two hundred years, in search of new lands, Frank Young's inherited pioneering spirit had lured him to this still wild land of mountains and desert. He had come to the little railroad town at the invitation of a cousin who had homesteaded in that area. It was his hope to find a suitable spot where he could safely establish a home for himself and wife and children. Might his future lie here, he wondered?

The railroad had come only a short time before, and the town, still building, was so new that the novelty of a train's arrival was an event. A crowd gathered at the station, curious to see what the iron horse had brought this day. Frank stood aside and put down his carpetbag. He was interested in people, and here was a new breed.

From the car ahead alighted a husky Indian and his squaw. He was dressed in what appeared to be a discarded cavalry uniform, though he wore no hat—only a band around his head. His hair was shoulder length. Moccasins were on his feet. Pinned to his coat was a piece of broad red ribbon, on which were crudely hand lettered the words "Scout—U.S. Army." The woman wore a voluminous dress, covering her completely from her head to her feet, which were bare. Her long hair hung in two braids down her back. She carried a heavy gunny sack, and walked behind the man as they moved toward three ponies held by an Indian boy. The three mounted; the woman received no help as she tied her sack to a battered saddle and scrambled topside.

Dominating the crowd in the station yard was a group of cowboys. They were similarly dressed in woolen shirts and copper-riveted denim pants, wide-brimmed Stetson hats, and silver-spurred boots. Each wore a holstered pistol. All seemed to be watching the detrainment expectantly. They broke into shouts as a newcomer drove up in a buckboard. Unlike the others, he was clean shaven, had a fresh haircut, and wore brand-new clothes.

"Damn near didn't make it," he said as he hurried toward the passenger coach. "One of the team fell lame—had to hitch up another. Where is she?"

One of the cowboys near the steps called out "All aboard!" in good imitation of a conductor's call. A look of shock came over the young man's face.

"Didn't she come?" he gasped.

One of the cowboys placed an arm around the young man's shoulders, facing him away from the car. This prevented him from seeing what all the others saw—the conductor appearing on the platform escorting a pretty young woman.

"Don't feel too bad, Johnny, old cuss," came the lugubriously soothing voice of the cowboy as he moved the young man farther away. "They's always other gals to be hooked, you know. She prob'ly figgered she just couldn't stand the sight of your ugly face day after day."

Others in the group crowded around, making soothing noises.

Johnny started to move toward his rig when he noticed all the other men grinning and removing their hats. He whirled.

Behind him he saw the conductor, also grinning, and beside him a blushing young woman. Johnny let out a whoop, seized her in a giant hug and spun her around and around.

"Bless your sweet little old Texas heart!" he shouted as he set her down, flushed and breathless. "I knew you'd come. This double-striped polecat here . . ." He turned, but the double-striped polecat had faded away into the group of shouting cowboys.

Johnny picked up the girl's bags and moved to the buckboard. They drove away followed by a barrage of pistol shots. As they passed close to where Frank was standing, he heard the young man say:

"The preacher will be at the church." Then, "The house is only one room, but we'll add to it as soon as . . ."

My father was to recall that remark at a later time.

Not far away was a two-story building built of pine lumber with the sign HOTEL painted on the side exposed to the station. He picked up his carpetbag and walked toward it.

In a fraction of an hour on Arizona soil he had observed interesting things. Arizona's spring climate was delightful. The land around the little desert station was wild, but there was a fascinating beauty in its wildness. All Indians weren't fighting the white man—he had seen some tame ones—and cowboys, surprisingly, had real human traits, he had noted.

He had seen the heartwarming sight of two young people ready to tackle the world with little but love, hope, and determination. He could compare that, Frank thought, to his own situation. With his wife Eva and two very young children, he was preparing to enter upon a new life with meager capital assets. But he did not doubt his possession of the other necessary qualifications.

Behind the reception desk in the hotel's small lobby sat a man with a very wide beam in a very large chair. The name "Humpty Dumpty" flashed into Frank's mind. His large head was bald as an egg. It resembled an egg, too, a cracked one. A scar ran down from above his right ear and ended near the nose. The weapon that made the cut had removed a small section of an ear, and in the healing of the cut, scar tissue had drawn down the lower eyelid, exposing a larger-than-normal area of white.

"Yeah?" the man said. "Want a room?"

They were interrupted by the sound of booted feet clattering down an uncarpeted stairway. A man dressed in black crossed rapidly to the door. With his hand on the knob he turned toward the desk.

"Hello, Fisheye," he said with a grin.

Frank had read of men capable of great speed in the use of knives and guns, and what he saw next convinced him that such tales could be true. The hand of the man behind the desk had been resting on the arm of his chair. Now his hand flashed upward to the back of his neck, and returned with a gleaming knife. With no perceptible pause, the arm snapped forward. The man in black tugged frantically at the door knob, which seemed unwilling to turn.

"No, Smitty, no!" The man yelled frantically, "I was funnin'!"

The knife clunked into the door frame near the man's head.

Smitty's hand continued its swift arc, grasping the grip of a big six-gun, which roared as a bullet splintered the door frame beside the knife just as the door came open. With a strangled yell, Smitty's victim dove to the board sidewalk. From his hands and knees he leaped to his feet and raced up the street, the clatter of his boots fading quickly.

Frank had stepped aside at the first flash of Smitty's knife. The knife and gun play had left him a little breathless, but his effort at nonchalance was successful.

"You missed him," he observed.

Something resembling a chuckle rumbled up from Smitty's throat.

"Missed him a-purpose," he said. "Just wanted to scare the bejayzus outa that crooked gambler. Told him never to call me that name. He'll know better than to cross this old Texas Ranger again."

"Reckon you've lost a roomer."

"Yeah. You want a room?"

"No—I'm here to visit a cousin of mine, Ed Kinnear. Can you tell me where he lives?"

"Five, six miles out." Smitty gave directions. "How you figger on gettin' there?"

"Shank's mare."

The glare turned on him from that big eye made Frank shiver.

"You don't look like a damn fool—don't you know nobody walks the desert? Indian country. Geronimo's out there. They still do some raidin'. Outlaws, too. Hire a horse. They's a livery corral on the way out. Got a gun?"

"No."

"Then get one! Gun shop up the street, two blocks. I'll take care of your bag."

An hour later, Frank Young, astride a horse, traveled southward along a little-used wagon road that wound its way through desert trees and brush. A cartridge belt was strapped about his waist, all loops filled. From the belt a holster was suspended, filled with a forty-five Colt revolver, much used but serviceable. He liked the feeling of safety the gun gave him. He knew quite a bit about guns. His father was a gunsmith; Frank had helped sight-in some of the rifles he had made and had done some pistol shooting, too.

As he traveled, the country became wilder. Frank became more alert as the sun sank low. Not far away were boulder-strewn hills, and beyond them, mountains where Apaches still had hideouts. He wondered why Ed Kinnear had chosen such a place to establish a home.

The sun was close to setting when a large, fort-like adobe structure came into view, half a mile away. This would be Ed Kinnear's place, he thought. He was close to the house when he sensed movement at the crest of a hill, less than a mile away. He drew up his horse for a closer look. Clearly seen was the silhouette of a man on horseback. A moment later he was joined by another rider, then another. They did not wear hats. They appeared to be looking his way. He put his horse to a gallop and was soon at the adobe house. He dismounted and knocked. After a minute of waiting, he shouted, then knocked again.

A little sliding panel at eye level in the heavy plank door slid back and a gruff voice demanded the visitor's identity. Then the door opened and Kinnear emerged, a rifle in his hand. He shook hands cordially.

"Take your horse to the corral at back," he said. "I'll open." He went back through the house.

The corral occupied a sizeable space, with adobe walls eight feet high. The rear end of the house formed a part of the enclosure. The double gate was of solid planking, secured on the inside by a heavy padlocked bar. Ed Kinnear opened the gate to admit Frank and his horse. Tin-roofed sheds covered stalls for horses and milk cows, a chicken roost, and a pile of baled hay. A pump supplied water to a drinking trough.

With Frank's horse watered and fed, Kinnear led his guest into the house. They had a hearty meal of beef stew, beans, and biscuits. While they ate, Frank told his host of the horsemen on the hill.

"Indians, no doubt of it," Kinnear said. "I knew a small band was near. They've raided some of the other ranchers' stock lately. They're after cattle and horses. They tried to break into my corral one night about a month ago, but they couldn't get past the padlocked bar. Reckon they may try again and it might be tonight. The cattlemen have organized a patrol, which helps, but small bands sneak in anyway."

"I read somewhere Apaches didn't raid at night."

"If that was ever true, they've changed their ways. White men's example, maybe."

Kinnear told how he had homesteaded this abandoned ground, taking a chance on the Indians being subdued in time for him to get a real stock-raising operation going. Mormons established a settlement here years before and built the big house as a protection against Indians. They built dams to store water for irrigation, but torrential rains washed them out. With the Indian menace hanging over them, they decided to search for a kinder place.

Kinnear showed Frank the interior of the house, most of which had been partitioned off into sleeping areas. In one corner a narrow stairway led to the roof.

"My feeling that we may have visitors tonight is growing," Kinnear said. "They know I have some of the best horses in these parts, and they want them. Well, I'll be ready for them."

A kerosene lantern lighted the way up the stairway. Climbing through a trap door, they emerged into a small tower that overlooked the corral. From this they stepped out upon the roof, which, like the floor below, was of tamped caliche, almost as hard and as impervious to water as concrete.

A moon in its second quarter illuminated the surroundings with a faint glow.

Inside the tower, a short ladder led up to a platform that offered an unobstructed view of the surroundings. Kinnear climbed up. After a short look around he called down softly, "There's movement out there. Up front." He came down, and stepped out beside Frank on the roof. An extension of the walls of the building formed a battlement all around with narrow, head-high slotted ports at frequent intervals. Hurrying to the front, Frank looked through one of these.

For about fifty yards from the house, the ground had been kept clear of brush, but beyond that there were clumps of mesquite and sage. Frank, too, was sure that there was movement out there.

"Now for our little party," Ed Kinnear said. From the shelter of the tower he drew a box that contained paper-covered cylinders about a foot long and thick as a man's wrist.

"These are cannon crackers I picked up at a Chinese store in Benson after the marshal barred them. The noise was so terrific that it scared horses two blocks away." He handed Frank several of the crackers, then ignited a stick of punk for each.

"The fuses on these bombs are cut short, so get rid of them quick after lighting. Look south. See that dark clump of mesquite out there? When they were here before they left some of their horses there. If they've done it again we'll try to stampede them. How's your throwing arm?"

"I've fired rocks a hundred yards," Frank replied.

Just as he spoke, a wild yelling came from the brush out front, followed by some rifle shots. Dim forms could be seen, always on the move.

"A diversion," said Kinnear. He hastily climbed the tower ladder where he could get a full view of the corral.

"There's someone down there," he said. "Let's go!"

He threw a bomb to land outside the gate. Frank threw his first bomb at the clump of mesquite. At its terrific roar, he heard the wild scream of a horse, then the pounding of hoofs.

Rushing to the front, Frank lit two more fuses and sent the bombs sailing out into the brush. Terrified yells followed and reverberated as Kinnear tossed more bombs into the night. They covered the ground on three sides of the house and beyond the corral.

"I don't think those 'Paches will come back," Kinnear surmised as they sat down before a fire in the big downstairs room. "They'll never forget that bombardment."

"Neither will I," Frank responded. "You know, Ed, I'm sure you've had the idea I might go partners with you out here, but I don't think this is the right place to bring Eva and the children."

"You're right. I thought Geronimo would be captured before this, but he's still out there. He can't last much longer, but . . ."

The next morning they inspected the grounds around the house. Inside the corral they found an iron bar, long and strong enough to have broken the lock. They found that the Indians' horses had broken their tethers with the exception of one frightened pony. Kinnear released it, and it made for the hills at a run.

In front of the house, the marauders departed in such haste that they left behind a rifle and two bows. One had jumped out of a moccasin. Atop a sage bush they found a dirty loin cloth.

"He went right through that bush," Ed Kinnear laughed. "You can have that for a souvenir."

When Frank declined it, Kinnear said he would tack it on his barn door.

In spite of Ed Kinnear's cheerful assurance that the Apaches would let him alone now, as Frank rode back to Benson he carried with him the uneasy feeling that his cousin knew better. After all, as he commented, those mountains out there still harbored Geronimo.

CHAPTER 2

The Desert

IT WAS THE MORNING OF THE SECOND DAY AFTER FRANK
Young left Benson that he arrived at Maricopa, twenty miles south of
Phoenix. This was still Indian country, but the local Indians, mostly
of the Pima and Maricopa tribes, had always been friendly to the white
man. Squaws in colorful dress sat on the ground as near as they could
get to the detraining passengers, displaying products of their native
skills: pottery, baskets, and beads.

There was no train to Phoenix; transport of passengers and freight
was handled by horse-drawn vehicles. Frank made arrangements to
have his trunk, re-checked from Benson, freighted to Phoenix, then got
aboard the stage, a long-bedded springed wagon fitted with a canvas
top and plank seats.

The road to Phoenix was rough, rutted, and dusty, except at the
Salt River crossing, where the water came up over the floor of the
wagon bed, causing the passengers to raise their feet and hold their
bags in their laps. This river, Frank knew, was the source of the water
that made the wide Salt River Valley bloom. After the stage arrived in
Phoenix, Frank took a room at a small boarding house. Fortified by a
quick meal, he eagerly sought the government land office.

What he learned there about land for homestead entry was discouraging. Desert land in the Phoenix area was of little value unless irrigation water could be supplied. A system of canals had been constructed, but due to the rapid influx of settlers, the land served by the canals was filed upon even before water could be delivered. It would probably be some time before any more canals would be dug, the land office recorder opined.

Was this to be the end of his dream for a new home in this fertile valley, Frank thought. Disheartened, he turned to leave when the recorder asked him to wait while he fumbled through some papers on his desk.

"This came today." He held up a letter. "A man named Wilkins writes he wants to release his homestead rights—for a price, of course. He's at the end of the Grand Canal, fifteen miles out."

Frank's hopes revived. He'd look at the place the next day. He enjoyed his trip next morning. The young gelding he rented at a livery corral was alert and easy-gaited. Maybe he could buy him.

Thirteen miles out, he struck desert country. He had passed the last house he would see until he reached his goal. Table flat, the desert stretched for miles with no barriers until it reached the far blue mountains that rimmed this Arizona valley. How different this was, he thought, from the lush rolling hills of central Ohio where he had been born and raised. The vegetation contained nothing here to match the little forests of oak and maple, hickory and walnut of his native state. Yet, this wild dry land was beautiful in its way.

Prior to leaving Ohio, he made a study of the wild things of the great Sonora desert, and could name most of the trees, bushes, and plants he saw. The thorny mesquite grew larger here, and was useful. Its hard wood made fine, durable fence posts and firewood, and its bean pods provided a rich food for livestock. Its cousin, the catclaw, was useful for the same reasons. There was the palo verde with its gray-green bark, which later would show masses of golden bloom.

Sagebrush grew vigorously, as did the creosote bush, commonly called greasewood. Gramma grass showed green in the open spaces, as did the gay wild flowers—lupines, showy primroses, verbena, and most striking of all, the golden desert poppies that grew in scattered, patterned masses.

Frank saw several varieties of cactus. This was not the preferred type of soil for the saguaro, giant of all cacti, as they grew best on rocky slopes, but Frank finally spotted one. Its fluted column towered thirty feet into the air. From the upper part of its gaunt trunk, two arms thrust outward and upward, as though in supplication, Frank thought.

Cottonwoods grew along the canal Frank was following, and a lush growth of watermoties, sometimes called arrow-weed, lined its banks, their slender stalks rising straight and lush.

With feed a-plenty this would be great country for wild life, Frank mused, and he was pleased with its abundance. To his amusement, a roadrunner kept pace with him. He put his horse to a gallop, and the bird not only kept pace but raced ahead. When Frank slowed his horse to a walk, the bird slowed too and gazed challengingly from orange-ringed eyes at this presumptuous invader.

A flash of gold high in a cottonwood tree marked a pair of orioles building a nest. The drumming of a woodpecker came clearly from another tree. Almost from under the horse's feet, a covey of quail rose and whirred away. Cottontail rabbits, feeding on roadside grasses, scurried to concealment in the brush. Later, he saw a long-eared jackrabbit stampede from a bush and speed away with enormous, streaking leaps, sailing over all obstacles without regard to their height. In quick pursuit rushed a coyote. As both animals passed from sight, the rabbit appeared to be gaining.

A row of cottonwoods marching southward came into view, plainly marking the course of a lateral ditch. This meant his destination was near. A short time later, he came to the canal's end, marked by a plank barrier that diverted the water into two ditches, one on each side. The flow was controlled by wooden gates, which could be raised or lowered. The ditch on the north side fed water to the land he had come to see. A heavy growth of weeds spread along its banks.

Westward, less than a quarter of a mile away, Frank saw the roof of a small building arising from a mesquite grove. He rode toward it. No fences barred his way. As he approached the building, he found it to be a one-room structure of unpainted boards and batts placed vertically, topped by a shake roof. Nearby, a team of horses was tied to a limb branching from a large mesquite tree. There was no barn or other outbuildings. A man emerged from the house wearing ragged clothing and sporting a scraggly beard.

"Mr. Wilkins?" Frank asked.

"That's me." After some preliminary discussion, he admitted he would release his homestead right if he could get what he wanted. Wilkins saddled a horse, and for two hours they rode around and over

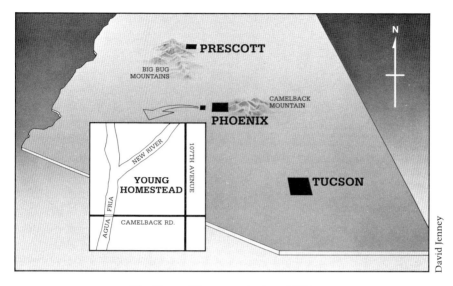

The Young Homestead, circa 1888

the quarter section. Frank noted that about forty acres on the west side lay against the channel of the Agua Fria River. They were sandy and stony and appeared to be useless for crops. There were about eighty acres of rich bottom land, and then the eastern forty sloped gently up to the level of the house.

The land here was of the type known as loess, deposited over the millennia by winds and leveled and firmed by rains. It was deep, as Frank could see by looking down Wilkins' uncurbed well. The size and vigor of the desert growth proved its fertility.

Wilkins had only the two horses Frank saw earlier, both mares of middle age, solid and sturdy. There were three cows, one a milker, and two heifer calves, a start for a herd. Rolling stock consisted of a farm wagon, a buckboard, and a buggy, all old.

A mowing machine, a rake, half of a double harrow, and a plow with a badly worn share concluded the list of farm machinery. It was all well worn. A miscellaneous assortment of battered hand tools lay in a packing box under a mesquite tree. A sadder lot of farm equipment Frank had never seen.

At the well, equipped with pulley and rope, Frank drew a bucket of water. It was cool and sweet.

He looked inside the one-room house and could barely repress a shudder. There had been no attempt at finishing, and all of the siding and beams were exposed, as were the shakes of the roof. Front and side doors were of pine lumber fastened together with cross batts, and equipped with rusty strap hinges and thumb latches. No locks—but no need. In a corner was a cot with rumpled blankets, and dirty clothing hung on nails driven into the walls. A table made of scrap lumber had a packing box for a chair, while other stacked boxes served as a cupboard. Close to the cupboard, and its meager supply of eating and cooking utensils and groceries, stood a rusty two-hole sheet-iron stove, its pipe protruding through the shakes of the roof. A coal oil can with the top cut out was the kettle and reservoir for hot water. In the yard by the side door, packing boxes held a wash pan and a side-opened five gallon coal oil can filled with water. The towel was a sugar sack opened at the seams. There was no outhouse. Evidently one of the close-by mesquite trees had been deemed adequate for a retiring room.

"What do you want for the relinquishment, livestock, and equipment?" Frank asked.

"I've been asking fifteen hundred, but you can have it for a thousand for a quick deal."

Frank shook his head. "Let's review what you have to offer. Forty acres of the allotment is sand. You have built no fences. No cleared land—the few acres you have watered and planted to alfalfa have the mesquite and catclaw stumps still in the ground. Ditching is incomplete, and the ditches you have done are in bad shape. The equipment is all old and in need of repair."

"Don't forget the house and well."

"Mr. Wilkins, I have a wife and two very young children. This building shouldn't be called a house—it's a shack and not fit for family living. As for the well, I would expect it to cave in at the first hard rain." He paused for a moment, then, "I'll give you five hundred for a relinquishment and a bill of sale for all livestock and equipment."

"I've already had a five hundred dollar offer from a feller name of Bill Boggs. Got a bad name. When I turned his offer down he threatened me—said if I valued my hide I'd be at the land office tomorrow morning to close the deal. I still said no—but he left me fidgety. I'd better not accept the same offer from another."

"Are there any debts or commitments of any kind against the property?"

"Nary a dime."

Frank took time to analyze the situation. What brought him to a decision was the thought of that eighty acres of rich bottom land.

"I'll raise my offer to six hundred," he told Wilkins. "But that's positively all. If you decide to accept, meet me at the land office at eight in the morning."

On his return trip to Phoenix he took a different route, a course north of the canal.

Because of the slope downward to the level bottom land, Wilkins had been able to get water on his land even to the northern line of his homestead without departing very far from the eastern boundary. Only a small triangle was isolated from the ground that could be irrigated.

The sun had passed its meridian when Frank turned his horse eastward. He wound through the desert on a leisurely course toward Phoenix. A mild breeze helped to alleviate the heat of the sun at his back. The desert was beautiful, and he frequently deviated to inspect trees or bushes or grasses. This would be wonderful cattle country, with the open range stretching to the far horizon. He must take advantage of it.

The air was sparkling clear. He could see mountains on all sides of him at varying distances. Far northward he could see, rising above all others, the snow-capped San Francisco Peaks, known locally as Four Peaks.

Clouds, snowy white, hung above the horizon. One of the masses of vapor resembled a ship in full sail. "Is that my ship coming in?" he asked himself. "If so, I christen thee Eva."

He took a sandwich from his saddlebag and ate it. A pair of broad-backed, low-slung badgers waddled across his path, not even bothering to look at him.

He felt himself falling in love with the desert. But would Eva, his wife, like it? Surely not without a comfortable dwelling. She had been reared in gentle ways, even though on the farm. Her father, George Lawrence, an English immigrant, had become a prosperous landowner; his four sons and four daughters had been raised in comfort. All who desired it were given college educations.

Eva, shy and sensitive, majored in art at Ohio Wesleyan University. Members of her family and her friends received her work: beautiful landscapes, portraits, and exquisite examples of china painting. Had he any right, he wondered, to bring her to this lonely place?

Then there were the two children, Lawrence LeRoy, two, and Elva Fay, one. This wild land was no place for babies.

Well, we'll see, he mused. I'll know more tomorrow.

Transforming a piece of raw desert to green cropland would be a grinding task. He knew this well enough, as his grandparents had been in a similar position. He was physically strong, and hard work had developed him into a man of tough fiber.

Traveling at a leisurely pace, he reached Phoenix in late afternoon. He returned the gelding to the corral, went to his room, cleaned up, then went to the dining room where he was served a thick T-bone steak, mashed potatoes with gravy, and flaky biscuits.

Though Frank suspected that he had seen the last of Wilkins, he was wrong. Wilkins was at the land office the next morning, but not alone. A roughly dressed, bearded man, almost as tall as Frank and heavier, was there too. At Frank's first sight of him he was shaking his fist in Wilkins' face.

"You're a goddam double crosser!" he was shouting. "You sold to me. I made a fair offer and you accepted—we shook hands on it."

Wilkins was half a head shorter than Boggs, but he didn't flinch.

"I never touched your dirty hand, yesterday or any other time. You offered five hundred dollars. I said no, and meant it." He turned to the watching recorder who, nodding toward Frank, said, "Well, I'm glad you two got together." He filled in a relinquishment blank, which Wilkins signed. Then a homestead entry blank was made out in Frank's name and signed. Frank paid the fee.

They walked down the street to a bank, where Frank deposited a draft and paid Wilkins.

"Your team is at the Jefferson Corral," Wilkins said. "I'm going down there now. This money will buy me a half interest in it."

Boggs, who had followed them to the bank, threatened them both with dire things.

"Mostly bluster, I reckon," Wilkins commented, "but we'd better keep our eyes open."

The next thing Frank did was to write Eva. He emphasized the fact that a tough time lay ahead.

"I can't send for you until I can build a better house than this miserable shack, which would be more suitable as a chicken house or a storeroom than a dwelling."

He felt great, he told her. The asthmatic condition which had been one of his reasons—or excuses—for migrating had almost disappeared in the short time he had spent in the marvelous Arizona air. He was ready for whatever might come.

As he hitched up his team at the corral, he remembered the gelding he had ridden the day before, and dickered for him. By stages, he got the price for the horse and saddle down from seventy-five to fifty-five dollars, and led him away behind the wagon. The mares of his work team bore the names of Dolly and Molly, Wilkins had said. Frank named the gelding Cholly.

At the corral Frank bought baled hay and rolled barley, the West's substitute for oats, picked up his trunk and carpetbag at the boarding-house, and bought a supply of groceries. He bought ammunition for his ten-gauge shotgun and forty-four Colt repeating rifle, which were in his trunk. He purchased cutting, grubbing, digging, and fencing tools to use with, or in place of, those left at the homestead.

On his way home he drove a westward course a mile south of the canal road. The last mile northward to his new home passed by his neighbor Snider's land. A small house, better than his own, rested upon it. No one was in sight.

The sun was still an hour high when Frank drove up to the door of his house. He was starting to unload when he sensed that he had a visitor. Suddenly, a man rode out of the mesquite grove and galloped toward him. At his belt was a pistol, in his right hand a rifle, pointed at Frank.

It was Boggs. "Get in the house," he ordered gruffly. It seemed best to obey. Boggs dismounted and followed closely.

On each side of the table was a box used as a chair. Boggs pointed to one of them.

"Sit down," he ordered. As Frank did so, Boggs leaned his rifle against the wall by the door and sat opposite Frank, his pistol ready at hand. Whiskey fumes enveloped him. He took a folded paper from his shirt pocket, spread it open, and shoved it across the table to Frank, tossing the stub of a pencil after it.

"Sign!" he ordered.

"What is it?"

"Relinquishment to your homestead claim. I made a fair and square deal with Wilkins, and because you offered him more money he ratted. I ain't goin' to let no goddam yellowbellied tenderfoot bust up my deal. Here's the five hundred I agreed to pay."

He tossed a roll of bills on the table.

Frank slowly counted the grimy bills.

"Ten dollars short," he said.

"You owe me a treat for the trouble you've caused me."

"But I paid six hundred . . ."

"That's your hard luck. Now sign that and quit stallin'!"

Frank signed, leaving the paper on his side of the table as he rose to his feet. As Boggs leaned over to pick it up, Frank's long arms shot out, his hands grasped the other man behind the head and slammed his face into the table, once, twice, three times.

As Boggs fought his way upright, Frank seized the edge of the table, tipped it up and slammed it against Boggs' chest, forcing him backward. He stumbled and fell, the table atop him. Cursing madly, he threw off the table and struggled to his feet, blood dripping from nose and lips, to find his own pistol pointing at him.

"It's your turn now," Frank said. "Get on your horse." He took the rifle away from the door.

Spitting blood and drawing upon a rather extensive vocabulary to express his opinion of the pilgrim who was stealing his land, Boggs nevertheless thought it wise to obey. He stumbled through the door and mounted.

"I'll leave your guns and money at the sheriff's office next time I go to town," Frank said. "You can pick them up there. Don't ever show your face around here again. I have guns, too, and know how to use them. Now ride!"

As Boggs paused to continue his harangue, Frank fired the pistol over his head. Putting spurs to his horse and bending low, he went away leaving a trail of dust.

Frank Young was basically a gentle man, and this encounter disturbed him deeply. But he didn't question his right to defend himself and property.

He was suddenly very tired, but there was still work to do. He unloaded the wagon, unharnessed the team, and watered his three horses at a small stock pond beyond the mesquite grove. This grove provided the only shelter for his livestock and the few chickens Frank discovered he owned. The cattle were penned in a small holding corral. He watered and fed them, found a pail at the house, and milked the milk cow.

By now the sun was setting behind the low range of mountains to the west, illuminating a bank of clouds with wildly gorgeous colors. There were a variety of silver, gold, red, orange, and purple shades. The brighter colors in this galaxy acted upon the normal blue of the sky to change it to a clear, bright green, an effect Frank had never before observed. I wish Eva was here with her paints and canvas, Frank thought. She would love a scene such as this.

The two small four-paned windows on either side of the shack were dirty and allowed only dim light into the shack. Frank lit a coal-oil lamp and made himself supper. He found a nest in the mesquites with fresh eggs in it, and had ham and eggs, fried potatoes, and coffee brewed in a lidless pot. He had had a pound of Arbuckle coffee ground at the grocer's. Before that was gone, he'd get himself a lap mill so he could grind his coffee fresh every morning.

Blankets were in the trunk. He spread them on the cot and after undressing, knelt.

"Oh Lord," he prayed "I thank thee for the manifold blessings thou hast bestowed on me and my loved ones. Though this land be harsh, help us to seek and find those beauties that will enable us to establish a happy home. Forgive my transgressions. Forgive those who would harm me, and point their way to a better life."

While he sought God's help, Frank knew that help must come in guidance, and that accomplishment would be the fruit of his own efforts. He must have a better house for his wife and children. He just couldn't expect them to endure the cold of winter in this miserable shanty.

On the thought that the Lord gave aid to those who were striving to do things for themselves, he got off the cot, took his cartridge belt and pistol from the trunk, and hung them on a nail in the wall beside the spot where he would lie.

The coyotes were tuning up for a welcoming serenade. The sounds came from all directions. Frank rather liked these wild songs of the little desert dogs, finding in their threnodic clamorings a wildness to match the vast sweeps of desert land.

He started to review in his mind the many tasks he must accomplish tomorrow, but exhausted, soon fell into a dreamless sleep.

CHAPTER 3

Hardscrabble in the Mesquites

FRANK WAS UP AT DAWN. A DISSONANT COYOTE CHORUS, seemingly very close, greeted him. He fed and watered the livestock, milked the cow, and turned the cattle out to graze, after giving them enough hay to make them realize this was home. He hitched his team to the wagon and started for town.

The first thing that must be done, he decided, was to fence his homestead to keep his own stock in and roving stock out. He made quick mental calculations. The land's two-mile perimeter would take six hundred and forty posts spaced one rod apart. He'd cut them himself, and in the process, clear his land of mesquite. Though barbed wire was dangerous to livestock, he couldn't afford woven fencing. Twenty-four quarter-mile spools—that would be around a hundred dollars for a three-strand fence. Cutting and setting the posts would be the big job. He'd have to hire someone to help him.

Upon his arrival in town Frank went straightaway to the sheriff's quarters. At a table sat a red-headed, lanky man wearing a deputy's badge. Frank placed the guns and the wad of money on the table.

"A man named Boggs left these at my ranch. I told him he could pick them up here."

A surprised look spread over the deputy's face. He scrambled to his feet.

"Sheriff!" he bawled. "Come here!" The sheriff hurried from an inner room. "Feller here says these are Bill Boggs' stuff."

"How'd you get 'em?" the sheriff demanded.

Frank explained briefly.

"Well, I'll be gol-danged to hell'n gone!" he exclaimed. "Bill won't call for 'em. Never heard of anyone takin' anything from Bill Boggs before."

Wilkins was at the corral, and Frank asked him if he knew of a good man he could hire.

"Maybe," he answered. "Juan!" he called out. A Mexican came out from the horse stalls. He was short of stature but sturdy of build.

"Juan Tapea," Wilkins introduced. "We've let him help around the corral for enough to eat on, but we don't need him."

Frank liked the looks of the man and quickly reached an agreement. A dollar a day, six days a week, and grub. Nothing was said about hours. It was understood a day meant dawn to dark.

From a niche in a pile of baled hay, Tapea quickly retrieved a half-filled gunnysack and bedroll and climbed into the wagon. It did not take the two long to load the wagon at a ranch supply house with half the barbed wire they would need, and other required fencing supplies.

"Me call Chappo," the new hand said as they took the road home. He spoke a mixture of Spanish and English. Frank saw the opportunity to learn some conversational Spanish. He found his knowledge of Latin helpful.

At home in late afternoon, Chappo found a nicely sheltered spot in the mesquite grove to put down his bed. Frank noticed he paused in a listening attitude several times while helping with the chores. As the two moved toward the house, Chappo paused again, facing west.

"You got *otros hombres, señor?*" he asked.

"No, I don't have other men. Why?"

"I hear the axe." He pointed west.

"You sure?"

"*Sí.* My ears good like cat."

Frank listened, but heard nothing. Soon Chappo said, "No more now, gone."

But early next morning while unloading the wagon, Chappo paused again, looked west, and said. "Axe. Two axe."

23

"We'll go see."

He put his rifle and shotgun in the wagon and they drove down the south line of the homestead. Frank could hear the axes now. Following the sound, they found two men vigorously swinging axes, cutting posts from the best of the mesquite trees which, favored by the rich bottomland, had grown to greater than average size. Frank alighted from the wagon.

"Good morning," he greeted. "My name's Young, new owner of this place. May I ask your name?"

"Snider. First ranch south," one of the men answered.

"And why are you taking posts from my land?"

"Wilkins' permission. Me and him has an agreement that I help clear the land, I get the posts." His voice carried a belligerent note.

Frank shook his head. "He told me emphatically that he was leaving no unfilled commitments, and I believe him. And you're not clearing the land—just taking the best of the timber and leaving the smaller limbs, stumps, and trash. Do you plan to clear these away?"

"That ain't what Wilkins said . . ."

"All right—let's go to town and ask him."

"Now see here, Young! I ain't goin' to let no damn tenderfoot . . ." he advanced on Frank, who actually laughed and strode forward to meet him. Snider stopped and backed up.

"As neighbors, we should be friends," Frank said. "But I'll not be robbed. Either we go see Wilkins or you'll get off my place and stay off."

"No!" The voice came from the man with Snider, who had produced a pistol. "You get off!"

Frank was wondering how he would cope with this new development when he heard Chappo's voice from the wagon bed.

"*You* will drop it, *señor*."

The man with the pistol turned to find himself looking into the twin barrels of a ten-gauge shotgun. He made haste to drop his weapon and back away, as did Snider.

Frank picked up the pistol, a small thirty-two caliber pocket gun. "What's your name?" he asked its owner.

"John Smith," the man snarled.

"I'll leave this gun at the sheriff's office, where you can pick it up. Now let's get on to town to see Wilkins."

"What for? He'd lie for you."

"Then let's count the posts."

There were three piles of posts in the disfigured mesquite grove. Snider made no move to check. Frank made quick work of the count. He had split and counted many a pile of fence rails back in Ohio.

"A hundred and fifty-nine, call it a hundred sixty." He took a purse from his pocket and counted out bank notes. "Here is eight dollars for your labor, at five cents a post."

With a look of surprise, Snider took the money.

"As neighbors," Frank went on, "it's stupid for us to be at odds. We have interests in common. Let's be friends." He held out his hand, which Snider took grudgingly. Frank feared his offer of friendship was of little effect.

They drove back to the house. At the corral they found four cotton-wood poles. Frank fastened a strip of cloth torn from a flour sack to the ends of each with baling wire. Then at each corner of the quarter-section tract they set a pole with its flag. It was mid-morning when they returned to the house. They filled canteens, took axes and grubbing hoes. The guns were left in the wagon.

"Maybe we'll get some cottontails," Frank said.

"*Señor*," responded Chappo, "you got the cartridge for the big gun?" He broke the lock on the gun, showing both cartridge chambers empty.

Frank threw back his head and laughed heartily.

"And you bluffed Smith with an empty gun?" he chortled.

"All same, scare hell out." Chappo grinned.

Their first job was to clear a path for the fence, wide enough for a wagon to pass through. There were trees to cut, brush to chop. Quite a few posts were added to Frank's already substantial stock left by Snider.

It took ten days, ending on a Saturday, before they were ready to set posts. The toil had been unceasing, sunup to sundown, with only a Sunday for rest. Chappo was a jewel, tackling each mesquite limb as though he had a personal grudge against it.

They went to town, loading the rest of the barbed wire and stocking up on other supplies.

Frank gave Chappo a five-dollar bonus, delighting the man. He promptly bought himself new work clothes, a straw hat with wide brim, and shoes. He needed them—he had worked his other clothes to tatters.

Frank called at the sheriff's office and turned in the pistol "John Smith" had surrendered. Taking one look at it, the deputy called for the sheriff, who came out of the inner office.

Identified by initials carved into the grip, the gun was one reported stolen by a prominent business man of the town. The initials were not "J.S."

The sheriff looked Frank over.

"Want to swear in as deputy?" he asked. "I can use a man good at disarming bandits."

When Frank described the man who had carried the pistol, the sheriff identified him at once as Jack Hawes, wanted for horse stealing. Boggs, he said, had not been seen.

Frank received two letters from Eva. She and the children were well. They longed for the day to come when they could be together.

"I don't agree with you that we can't all live in a one-room house. We expect inconveniences to begin with. My folks were pioneers, as well as yours, and both of us are familiar with the hardships attached to settling in a new land, and if you can stand it, I and the children can." Frank was finding that there were things yet to learn about his wife's character and resolve.

At a supply house he found a used cast-iron cooking stove with four holes on top, a warming hearth and an oven large enough to bake four loaves of bread. He took it home with him, and that evening he and Chappo had hot biscuits with butter made by shaking sour cream in a fruit jar.

Monday morning they began making the fence. They loaded posts on the wagon, and dropped them off in the cleared path. Then one of them dug holes, while the other set posts and tamped the earth around. Five of Frank's long strides measured a rod. They would occasionally switch positions. They set up to fifteen posts an hour without exhausting themselves. Wire was strung by reeling it out from spools in the wagon bed, then tightened with a wire stretcher and stapled.

On the eleventh day after the first post was set, the fence was finished. Six miles of shining barbarous barrier wire surrounded the desert homestead. Cross-fencing would come later.

Frank and Chappo took a double holiday, spending Saturday in town.

Two more letters from Eva. Since Frank insisted, she said, she would wait until fall to come to him, but no longer.

Frank bought some seed, wheat and alfalfa. He picked up some used chairs, and would make more household purchases before Eva came.

It was late for planting, but he sowed some alfalfa seed to supplement the scant stand Wilkins had left among the stumps. He also sowed some wheat, as it might help to shade the new alfalfa seedlings.

It was after sundown when Chappo came running to the house. "*Señor! Señor!*" he cried excitedly. "The wheat . . . the quail . . ."

Frank grabbed his shotgun and hurried down to the field. He was startled by a sight he eventually was to see repeated often. Hundreds of quail were busily scratching up and eating the wheat he had planted.

He fired both barrels of his shotgun into them, and got enough quail for breakfast. But they were back next morning. He built a framework for a scarecrow and dressed it up with Chappo's discarded clothing.

"It's going to work," he said the next morning when he saw but few quail about. But he changed his mind the following morning when he saw a cock quail on guard duty atop the dummy's hat.

The alfalfa seed was too fine for the quail to bother with. Despite the birds' industry, a light stand of wheat germinated, to be used later for chicken feed.

With the arrival of June came heat, such heat as Frank had never experienced. His thermometer, before the month ended, reached as high as one hundred and twenty degrees inside the house. But with the very low humidity it wasn't so bad as one might imagine. Chappo didn't seem to mind it. Frank moved his cot outdoors at night.

After cleaning all ditches, Frank and Chappo went to work clearing land. The larger mesquite and catclaws had been cut for posts, but there were many smaller limbs to be cut into firewood. The trimmings were piled for burning. Then the stumps, which also would be cut up for firewood, were grubbed out. It was grinding work, but with twelve-hour days they made good progress.

This work well under way, Frank took time out to do other needed things. He had persuaded Eva that she must not come until fall so that she would escape the terrific heat, the force of which he did not minimize.

Since there were no shade trees around the house, he planned shade in another manner. He cut poles from the cottonwoods along the canal bank, and encircled the shack in a ten-foot perimeter, using other poles fastened horizontally at the top to support a thatch of leafy watermoties, also from the canal banks. The pole and thatch structure he called "the shade," a name it retained.

He bought two brood mares, more cows and calves, and a young bull. Now his herd was started and would grow rapidly from year to year, he hoped.

His dwindling capital would not permit the building of the new house of his dreams, but he bought lumber and built an extension at the back to match the "main" room in size. The roof sloped down from the eight-foot eaves of the shack to a bare six feet. He moved the cook stove and table into the new room.

He built the needed cross-fence, allowing his livestock to browse half the ranch without invading crops growing on the other half.

He and Eva agreed on early October for her arrival. Before that time came, Chappo asked for leave.

"I want to go see *mi esposa*—my wife in Sonora—and give her some money. But I will be back if, *por favor*, you want me work some more." Chappo was no spender. He had over one hundred dollars in his jeans.

"You come see me when you get back," Frank told him. He didn't want to lose as good a worker as Chappo as long as he could manage to pay him.

Frank had found no opportunity to become acquainted with his neighbors, except for the unfortunate meeting with Snider. Out here anyone who lived within ten miles was considered a neighbor, he knew.

On a Saturday when in town he had his hair cut, his beard trimmed, and indulged in a twenty-five cent bath, in a real tin bathtub—hot water, soap, and towel furnished. Much more comfortable than the tub at home, which served for both bath and laundry. Sunday morning, he took a suit from his trunk and dressed for church. He saddled Cholly and rode to the little school house, known as the West End School, which served as a community center.

He arrived early, before the men's Bible class had assembled. A man named List took him in hand, and began introducing him as "the man who took Bill Boggs' guns away." Frank deplored this publicity, and was surprised to learn he was quite a celebrated figure in the community.

As the Bible class adjourned, the preacher, one of several Phoenix ministers who intermittently supplied his services to the West End pulpit, was introduced to Frank by List who mentioned the Boggs affair. The preacher was not favorably impressed. He looked upon him, Frank thought, as though he had done an evil thing.

"Did it occur to you," he said, "that love conquers where violence fails?"

"No," Frank answered. "Would you have thought of how to use love while looking down a gun barrel?"

"Yes," answered the preacher, as he turned to his pulpit, which was usually the school teacher's desk.

A few good voices made up a small choir. The man of God preached a turgid sermon about sin, hellfire, and the power of love over hate. When he finally closed he said, "We have with us this morning one whose name is known to most of us, but who has not visited the church before. Mr. Young, I invite you to offer the closing prayer."

Frank responded fervently. His closing words seemed to bring unusual quiet to the audience.

"We beseech thee, oh Lord, to bestow thy divine blessing on each and every one of us. Forgive us our shortcomings, and lead us along a path from which the stones of sin and temptation have been cleared. Bless the preacher who has traveled so far along a dusty road to bring us the Word. May he be forgiven for the temptations which may beset him, and may he be given a clear understanding of the meaning of love as it burned in the heart of Christ. Amen."

The preacher neither thanked nor even looked at Frank as he took his departure. He got a different reaction from List, who seemed to speak for the other men present.

"I liked your prayer, even though the preacher didn't," he said. "I heard what he said before the service. You did a great thing with Boggs—it would have been a good thing if you'd shot him. Did you know he's in the Yuma penitentiary?"

"I hadn't heard that."

"Yes—robbed the Prescott stage. Our sheriff got him—I heard someone say he was wearing Boggs' own guns when he caught him."

On the ride home he pondered over his first attendance at a church service since leaving Ohio. It left something to be desired. He hadn't intended to arouse the reverend's resentment, even though his had been aroused over the reference to the Boggs' affair and his evident disapproval over the way he had handled it. That was nonsense. Frank's definition of love didn't include the word pacifism, nor the "turn the other cheek" philosophy when one's life might be in danger. Francis Asbury Young was a religious man, with a practical view of the Bible's teachings. He had been named for one of the most famous of early American divines. His grandfather had been a minister, his brother was a minister, his wife's brother was a minister. He felt secure in his views.

The following days went by so fast they seemed to blur in Frank's mind. The days were becoming shorter and he paid no more attention to "daylight to dark." He made his nights very short. In daylight hours he continued work on ranch projects—building new ditches, grubbing more stumps, repairing the house—it was an endless labor. By the light of coal-oil lamps at night and early morning he worked indoors, doing what he could to make the house a little more liveable. He built an outhouse by moonlight—he wouldn't have believed until he came to Arizona that the moon could give so much light. He could read a newspaper by it.

He gave his old farm wagon a coat of paint; it looked better, but not much. He took the spring seat from the buckboard and put it in the bed of the wagon for the children.

The day of his family's arrival finally came. The stage was scheduled to reach Phoenix around noon. Waiting, Frank wondered and worried about Eva's reaction when she encountered the reality of the shabby little house in its wild desert setting. He had in his letters tried to prepare her, even attempting to impart a feeling of romance to his descriptions of the wildness and solitude of this land so far away and different from anything he had known.

These things were still in his mind when the stage arrived at the station. Yes, Eva was there! She occupied the first seat behind the driver; Lawrence and Fay were on either side. Fay slept, her head in her mother's lap, while Lawrence was engrossed in observing the strange sights, sounds, and people.

Eva was anxiously looking around, looking for her husband, whom she did not recognize. Frank hurried up, and addressed her.

"Pardon me, madam, I'm looking for a young woman named Eva. Could that be you?"

Startled, Eva looked at him. She said, "But where . . ." Then she looked into his eyes, and gave a little shriek.

"Frank—oh Frank. I had begun to be frightened."

Her arms were around Frank's neck as he helped her down. They stood a few moments in a long embrace. Frank had been away so long that his children scarcely remembered him, and they shrank away from the bearded stranger. It didn't take long, though, before they succumbed to his gentle voice; in short order, they were friends.

There were marks of weariness in Eva's face. It had been a hard journey with the children, their only beds the car seats. Frank loaded Eva's two suitcases and the large basket that her mother had packed with food for the journey into his own wagon, then drove his family to the boardinghouse where he was already known. They all enjoyed a good meal and Eva and the children had baths and naps, while Frank picked up Eva's trunk and bought supplies.

On the way home Frank continued to refer to Eva's home-to-be in an apologetic way, until she stopped him.

"Don't you know," she said, "that I'd be happy in a hut so long as you were with me?"

Frank's voice was husky as he responded, "Thank God for giving me you."

And so Eva and Frank Young and their children embarked on a pioneering journey that was to bring them happiness and sorrow, joy and tragedy.

CHAPTER 4

Longhorns and Spuds

THEY ARRIVED AT THE HOMESTEAD IN LATE AFTERNOON. Frank continued to worry about the homecoming, fearful that Eva's reaction to the first sight of the house would be shock. It was such a drab little place, with its unpainted boards and unsightly brush shade surrounding it.

With wonderment, Frank noted that Eva's expression of serenity did not change. She looked about with interest, the little half smile that normally hovered about her lips still there.

Frank helped his wife and children down from the buckboard and into the house through its battered, outward-swinging front door. He turned to Eva, removed his hat, and bowed.

"Welcome to my castle," he said, unable to dispel a sardonic note.

"It's our home," Eva responded, "and we'll make it a happy one."

He hugged her, and went out to unload Eva's trunk and bags, then unharnessed and fed the team, fed the chickens, and milked the cow.

Meantime, Eva gave the two rooms a careful inspection. They had a good bed, and that was important. She feared Frank had spent too much on it, though. She would be able to curtain it off. At the foot of the bed was a roomy crib, which for the time being would do for the two little children. At one corner, a space had been curtained off for a clothes closet. In another was a series of shelves for books and magazines, writing materials, and gadgets. In an opposite corner was a custom-made piece of furniture, a three-cornered affair designed for economizing space. Its several shelves were open. I can display some of my hand-painted china there, Eva thought. Completing the furnishings were three chairs, a rocker and two straight backs.

Seeing the wide cracks between the shrunken boards of the floor, she decided some rugs should be placed there as soon as possible.

Passing through the door into the second room, she saw a round table of Frank's own construction, made of new redwood lumber. It would seat six, eight in a pinch. There were some chairs, battered but serviceable, and two benches. Frank had built two high chairs for the children.

There were shelves for utensils, nails on which to hang the skillets and other items with handles, a wood box, and a box with hinged top for flour and sugar sacks. On the back side, where the roof slanted down to only six feet from the floor, spikes had been driven in to serve as racks for the rifle and shotgun and to hang up Frank's pistol and gun belt.

The side door opened out to the west. Looking out, Eva saw a bench with a wash basin on it and a five-gallon can of water and a cake of soap. Hanging on the wall was a large washtub and a washboard.

She saw something else—a gorgeous sunset, unlike anything she had seen in Ohio. Banks of low clouds were shot through with fantastic colors. Frank came in from his chores and put his arm about her waist.

"It's beautiful," she said. "It makes me wish I could paint it."

"Did you bring your paints?"

"Yes, I'll have to get them out."

They ate their supper by the light of a coal-oil lamp. Eva found the little stove, stoked with mesquite wood, very efficient. Frank had the best meal of his Arizona career, with sirloin steak, hash brown potatoes, hot biscuits, and canned green peas and peaches. Among his livestock purchases had been a Jersey milk cow, and now it pleased Frank to watch the children eagerly drink her rich, warm milk.

After the dishes had been done and the children placed in their crib, Frank and Eva discussed plans for the future. Holding nothing back, Frank told of the favorable as well as the unfavorable features of life in the desert.

"It will be hard on you and the children," he told Eva. "It isn't too late to leave and look for a place nearer civilization—a Phoenix man offered to buy at a price that would allow us to clear a thousand dollars."

"Let's not give up," Eva advised.

"There are good prospects here. We have some excellent land. We are right on the edge of the open range, which stretches away for miles, with no restrictions on grazing. I figure to work toward a herd of two hundred cattle, with a minimum of winter feeding. We'll raise good horses, too. When the clearing is done, I'll have close to a hundred acres of fine land to plant to alfalfa and other things. Water may be a problem. We can expect years when there will not be enough."

"I like the plan," Eva said. "I especially like the idea of free grazing."

Frank got out his notebook and showed Eva the plan he had sketched for a new house.

"This shows six rooms," he said. "Sitting room, dining room, kitchen, and three bedrooms. We can start with less if we have to, and add on later." Frank paused, remembering the young cowboy's remarks to his betrothed on Frank's first day in Arizona. He continued, "And on three sides we'll have screened porches to keep out insects and to provide sleeping space in hot weather."

"That looks wonderful!"

"I'm thinking of making the walls of adobe if I can locate some good clay soil. Adobe brick, if made right, will last for centuries. I'll make molds for bricks twelve by eighteen inches, and the thick walls laid with such bricks will keep the house warm in winter and cool in summer. I can hardly wait to get at it."

"It will be marvelous to have such a home," Eva responded. "But this will do fine until more money comes in. Let's get more cattle first."

"You're right, of course. I hope to be situated some day so we can get a fine grade of beef cattle, but right now these long-horned animals will do, as they can live on a range where the heavy breeds would starve. If only I had more land! I could file on the quarter section to the north as a timber claim, but that means a well and pump. But the house first, of course."

"We'll wait for that—I like the idea of a large herd of cattle."

It was a relief to Frank that Chappo returned the following week, having walked from town. The happy disposition with which Frank had become familiar seemed to have sunk without a trace.

34

"Welcome back, Chappo," Frank greeted. "Did you have a good trip?"

"No, *señor*." Chappo stared at his feet. *"Mi esposa—"* There was a break to his voice. "My wife, she not wait for me. She go with another man."

Frank felt sorry for this gentle man. He deserved better than that.

"I like work for you now," Chappo offered.

"If you want to stay here this winter, I'd be glad to have you—but I can't pay you much. A place to stay and your grub . . . then next spring, maybe a steady job. Maybe I can give you a little money, too."

"Gracias, señor. Está bueno."

Eva adjusted herself well to her new surroundings, and joined eagerly into a continuing discussion of their plans. Her well-concealed fear of the desert gradually departed. The nervousness she had felt at the coyote serenade that greeted her on the night of her arrival slowly subsided. It disappeared completely after an incident that first terrified her, then set her to laughing.

One morning, after Frank and Chappo left to continue clearing land, she took a pail of kitchen scraps and walked out to the mesquite grove to feed them to the chickens. Her arrival was noiseless, and suddenly she saw a coyote slinking toward the chicken pen. Her heart seemed to rise to her throat, choking a shriek to a gurgle. The coyote heard it, and swiftly turned his head in her direction. Eva regained at least a part of her voice.

"Shee!" she managed.

The coyote left in such a hurry that all Eva saw of him was a gray streak. When she recovered her composure she was able to laugh. Frank had been right, after all. Coyotes were cowards. Never again did she feel fear of them.

That winter, Frank and Eva continued to plan. To Frank's satisfaction, Eva had continued to adjust well to their rough existence, and was an eager partner in their discussions.

Eva insisted that they put all thought of the new home in the background until more money was coming in. She could help. They would increase the flock of hens and egg production. At Phoenix stores, farm products could be traded for groceries on a better basis than for cash. For instance, a pound of butter would buy a pound of Arbuckle coffee, and sometimes even more than that. There was always a market for eggs. They could sell cockerels at the restaurants, and they themselves could use hens past their prime. Chicken and dumplings every Sunday, maybe? Frank could raise enough grain for the flock. And wonderful bran was made by the flour mill at Tempe, across the river from Phoenix. The shorts (wheat germ and rough flour) were left in, resulting in a product loaded with nourishment, perfect as a hot mash for the hens.

Thus, in time, Eva's poultry and dairy products contributed a welcome addition to the income from the homestead in these beginning years. Meanwhile, the herd was increasing and clearing of the bottom land went on.

One problem that never ended was the uncertainty of the supply of irrigating water. Being at the very end of the canal was a disadvantage. In spite of the efforts of the ditch boss—officially known as the *zanjero*, a name locally pronounced "sankerro"—to apportion the water supply, those located on the upper reaches of the canal made sure they weren't going to be the losers.

All the irrigation canals headed on the Salt River, and diversion of water into them was accomplished by the construction of impermanent dams, using materials at hand: rocks, poles, and brush. Heavy floods would destroy these flimsy affairs, and as a result, there would be periods when no water flowed in the canals. This didn't matter so much if the valley had good winter and spring rains, but it might be serious if the dams were lost in summertime.

Water was sold by the "inch," which was equal to a small fraction of an acre foot and measured by the size of the aperture through which the water passed. Being at the very end of the Grand Canal created a troublesome problem, as at times the flow of water was so small that there was not enough for division. When this happened, each rancher had to take the entire flow on a time basis.

The *zanjero* would notify them as to how long the water would be turned down to them. Dividing this reported time evenly proved difficult, as the flow often remained on a dwindling basis long after the final half time period. This was fine from Snider's point of view, but not from Frank's since Snider had been assigned the second period. Frank insisted on an alternation of the half-time periods. No, Snider had started as second man, and he'd stay that way. When the argument got ugly, Frank called in the *zanjero*, who agreed that Frank's plan was more equitable. Together they found Snider, who couldn't give a sensible reason for not accepting the plan.

"That's the way we started," he said, "and that's the way it'll have to go on. Young didn't kick when we made the arrangement, which we both understood would be permanent."

"You are lying, Snider," Frank said. "No permanency in the arrangement was even hinted at."

Snider was plainly still burning over the matter of the posts.

"Young's way is the only fair way," the *zanjero* said. "That's the way it'll be."

Snider was furious. "I ain't goin' to let a goddam tenderfoot . . ."

"Oh, shut up!" commanded the *zanjero*. He pulled something from his pocket and showed it to Snider. "This is a deputy sheriff badge, and I have the power to arrest."

He scribbled in a notebook, and handed a sheet to each of the men.

"That's my order," he said. "Obey it. It's a long way down here, and I don't want to have to come back."

Snider's hatred seethed, but he bottled it up. It would be a long time before it would be displayed again.

Frank and Eva had found little difficulty in accommodating themselves to the mild winter, even in a house so well ventilated. In the materials that had been freighted from Ohio were heavy clothing and warm bedding, and both parents and children kept snug and comfortable even in windy and rainy weather. It never snowed; sunny days prevailed. The only ice they saw was a thin coating in such places as the edges of the stock ponds and on the water bucket outside the door.

Frank and Chappo continued their clearing chores, though never at the pace they had set that first spring and summer. The pile of stumps near the house grew higher and higher. Frank regained some lost weight and, best of all, the asthmatic condition that had encouraged him to go west had disappeared for good.

As winter traveled its temperate path toward spring, Frank began to cut up the dried-out mesquite stumps. It took strong arms and determination to reduce a gnarled and heavy hardwood bulk to stove-size pieces, but Frank had both, plus a sharp and heavy axe.

"A couple of these chunks will keep the stove hot all night," he had told Eva. His prediction proved to be accurate when the chilly nights came. In the light of a new day, it was comforting to find a kitchen with the chill removed and five gallons of warm water on the stove.

By the time spring arrived, Frank had another five acres ready to plant. He became obsessed with the idea that he could raise potatoes, a product that was shipped into Phoenix from outside. Upon inquiry at grocery stores, he was told that it was too hot in the valley to raise "spuds," the common name for them. Several had tried it and failed. But he hoped to prove them wrong. So he had a sack of seed potatoes shipped to him, and he cut them up and planted in March. They came up fine, and the plants flourished.

"They are so large I'm worried," Frank told Eva. "I wonder if I've given them too much water?"

The sweltering heat of early summer checked the growth of the vines. Curious, he began to dig. His disappointment was keen. Two things were very wrong. The potatoes were too small to be marketable, and they were scabby.

"I'll keep trying," Frank insisted. "Earlier planting and less water may be the answer. Anyway, we won't have to buy potatoes for awhile."

When the spuds were sorted, they had several sacks of them, two sacks of which were of edible size. The little stuff would go to the cows and chickens. Eva fed the family fried potatoes, mashed potatoes, boiled potatoes, baked potatoes, potato salad, and potato soup.

They had a good crop of spring calves, and Frank bought several bull calves from a dairy. In another year he would have marketable beef. Frank registered two brands, one in his name, the other in Eva's. His was a monogram of his initials, and was seldom used, as it was too complicated and large. Eva's brand was simple—a Coptic L. This resembled a Z, with the downstroke slanted to the right, and on the left of this downstroke, a hook, the point down.

When asked to describe this brand, the statement that it was a Coptic L didn't mean a thing to other ranches and buyers. Considerable imagination was used in describing brands—such as the famous hashknife, rocking chair, pot hook, and so on. A slanting downstroke, a "slash"; a horizontal stroke, a "bar"; a square, a "box." A letter or figure on its side is "lazy." The most common of the names by which Eva's brand was known was the "Z hook," but such names as "leanin' Z hook," "crazy Z hook," "stumblin' Z hook," or "tumblin' Z hook" were also used. Stockmen also registered earmarks. The one used on Frank's herd was "right ear, split; left ear, over-slope and under bit."

It was in April that Eva disclosed to Frank a piece of news that aroused in him a potpourri of emotions. There was joy that the third child they had wanted was soon to be; sorrow that the woman he loved should pass her pregnancy in such a barren place; chagrin that he had failed to provide the means for a new home; fear because they lived so far from a doctor; finally, happiness. Eva scoffed at all his doubts and glowed because she was to be a mother again. She had never intended to stop before she had the complete family she thought a requisite for pioneer life. She was one of six. That was the way of the times.

"This one should be a boy, if the sequence you have established is followed," Frank said.

"But we'll love just as much whoever comes," Eva responded.

As the summer came down upon them, Frank saw that, despite Eva's never-failing cheerfulness, the heat was weakening her. He hitched Cleopatra—Cleo for short—to the buggy and drove her to Phoenix to consult Doctor Battin, who was to be their family doctor from then on. He strongly urged that Frank take her north to the pine country. He named a place—Big Bug Canyon, south of Prescott. Frank never had a thought of ignoring the doctor's advice. It would be a squeeze, but he would make it.

He had Chappo drive three of his best yearling calves to a Phoenix buyer. He bought hoops and a canvas cover, two canvas cots, and canvas for bedrolls. With boxes of food, some five-gallon cans of water, and needed utensils and tools, they headed north early in August, driving their best work team.

They made connection with the Black Canyon Stage route between Phoenix and Prescott, crossed Deer Valley with its forest of saguaros, and went past a large flat area covered with cholla cactus, their tufts of porcupinelike thorns glowing with seeming incandescence in the afternoon sunshine.

On the second day, the road led them into the mountains; it narrowed to one-way traffic, with occasional turn-outs where vehicles could pass. Mesquite and cactus merged with juniper and manzanita. On the evening of the third day, they were in Big Bug Canyon, camped in a grassy vale with towering ponderosa pines all around them and a little spring-fed stream close at hand. Their valley home lay in desert heat eighty miles away, while the air in this mile-high spot was delightfully cool and refreshing.

Eva had endured the trip well. Both she and Frank were able to enjoy the first complete relaxation they had had since coming to Arizona. They marveled at the exuberance displayed by Lawrence and Fay in their explorations of this mountain paradise. It was hard for them to leave after three weeks. It had been the most delightful vacation that either of them had ever spent.

Chappo had been faithful in his attention to the ranch, and once back, Frank and Eva reluctantly fell into their established routine, helped by the cooler weather that came in September.

Eva began to prepare for the birth of her third child. The treadle-operated sewing machine Frank brought her had extra duty now.

Frank was worried about Eva's care when her time came. Suppose he didn't have time to get her to a doctor? It was fifteen miles to Phoenix—even with his best buggy horse, it would take around two hours to make the trip. Eva didn't seem concerned about it. Frank would meet the situation, she knew, whatever the eventualities.

Late in September, Frank drove Eva to Phoenix to see Dr. Battin. After his examination, he pronounced her in perfect condition and said he believed that she should have a normal delivery. He opined they could anticipate the event in time to get her into town.

"But," persisted Frank, "suppose something should happen which would make it necessary for the birth to be at the ranch?"

"Then you would have to roll up your sleeves and go to work."

Frank shivered at the thought. He proceeded to question the doc exhaustively as to what would have to be done. Dr. Battin answered his questions in detail, and loaned him a book on obstetrics to study.

Frank hoped that he would never have to use what he had learned. He cautioned Eva often to use restraint in the pursuit of her household duties.

"Of course," she would smile, and go right on working.

It was after midnight in late October, 1887, when Eva awoke Frank from a deep sleep. She told him she believed her time had come. Frank reacted with stunned silence. What he feared was about to happen.

Dear God, help me! he thought. He leapt out of bed, lit several lamps, built a fire, put on kettles and cans of water to heat, laid out supplies: basins, soap, and towels. Then, after again calling upon God to help him, he went to work.

It was a normal birth, though a little more difficult than with Lawrence and Fay. Was this a portent? Was this child to be different?

"I'm glad it's a boy," Eva said. "We'll have another girl next time and keep up the sequence until we have . . ."

"Whoa there!" said my father. "Let's take care of what we have first."

Thus, on that cool October morning, I, Herbert Vernon Young, had a window opened upon a new world, a world both beautiful and ugly, the only one I was to know until a decade had passed. It was a world vividly recalled because there were few things from the outside to clutter my memory.

I was healthy, restless, and loud. My mother recovered quickly from her ordeal, and hit her regular stride in a week's time.

My father, the recent event enhancing his worry over the inadequacies of the little house in the desert, began working harder than ever while planning the best way to increase his income. He couldn't get potatoes out of his mind. His rich land, water, and a climate that should be favorable if the planting time was properly chosen, ought to produce a good crop. He ordered seed for an acre, and when the alfilaria and gramma grass first began to show green in February's warming days, he planted.

In two weeks, the plants began to show. He irrigated just enough to keep the ground reasonably moist, avoiding saturation. He bought cultivators, one with harrow teeth to keep the soil between the rows pulverized to hold an even state of moisure, another to deepen the furrows when it was necessary to keep the water away from the plants.

He worked, waited, and worried. The kind of crop he got from that acre of land might mean the difference between a real house or a continuation of life in the shack.

When the vines died as summer heat intensified, Father and Chappo started to dig. The result was exhilarating. When they finished the first long row, they could look back on a dozen sacks of smooth potatoes, most of them of marketable size. He felt his future to be safe. Perhaps the time would be short until the new house could be built.

Is it a good or bad thing that man cannot foretell his future?

CHAPTER 5

Toil and Tears

FATHER FOUND A READY MARKET FOR HIS SPUDS IN PHOE-
nix, and the several tons he sold brought welcome cash. He had high
hopes and, after his last load had been marketed, told Mother they
could now begin to make definite plans for the new home.

"I'll have you out of this hut in another year," he declared.

"But Frank," Mother responded. "Won't that mean giving up our
plan to file on the land to the north?"

Father paused to think that over. Reluctantly, he admitted the
point was well taken. He had heard rumors that another canal would
be built, which might eventually be able to furnish water to the land
he wanted. Someone might file a homestead entry any time. He had
used up his homestead rights, leaving the filing of a timber claim his
only recourse. And that would mean a well and a pump.

It seemed hopeless. He scratched his head and combed his beard
with his fingers.

"We'll need that land," he declared. "If we're going to keep expand-
ing our herd. But you . . ."

"Come, come, Frank. I've told you how I feel."

"Yes, I know. You'd sacrifice every comfort to help me achieve what I'd like to have."

He got up from his chair and for a few moments paced back and forth on the splintery floor. Finally, he went to where Mother was seated, tipped her chin, and kissed her.

"Let me tell you what I think of you," he said, his voice husky. He proceeded to do so at some length.

The thing to do, they later decided, was to file on the quarter section as a timber claim entry and start a well, as evidence of good faith.

The ninth decade of the nineteenth century was nearing its close when my father received a letter from his mother stating that she was coming to visit him and his family. This was welcome news, as his surviving parent held a high place in the hearts of both her son and his wife.

When Father met his mother at the stage station, it was obvious that the trip had strained her endurance. Her once-strong body had wasted, and her face was thin and drawn. It was clear that a serious malady, in its embryonic stages when he had seen her last, had made serious inroads. From a hint or two she loosed, Father deduced that her urge to make this trip was based on a fear that unless she made it then, it might never be made at all. She had come directly from Iowa where she had been visiting her oldest son, Graham.

Maria Weed Graham Young showed no dismay at the undeveloped condition of my father's homestead, as he had feared she might. She was no stranger to pioneering. Her parents had migrated from Vermont to Ohio at about the same time my father's grandfather had. Their lives had also been hard.

During the early part of her stay the mild, clean spring air seemed to have a beneficial effect. Father gave her a buggy trip into the desert and her interest in the desert growth was keen. She especially enjoyed the bursts of bloom that covered the desert floor in places.

Father showed her the land he longed to acquire as a timber claim, and the tract to the west of it. He explained how his hunger for more land conflicted with his companion desire for a decent house for his growing family.

"If you can endure to keep on living as you do awhile longer, I recommend that you get the land if you can. I have seen land multiply in value back home. It will do the same here. But, Frank, couldn't Eva file on another homestead?"

"No, only one to a family."

"You spoke of a timber claim. Could I file on one?"

"Yes, you could."

"Then couldn't you and I together file on the half section you want?"

"We could."

"Then we'll do it! I'll assign my rights to you."

"I'll have to provide water."

"Secure the land first. Then, if you have to give it up, you won't be out much."

Although he worried where this new venture might lead him, my father took the necessary steps to file on the half section of land in his and his mother's name. He was happy to learn that there would be no legal bar to having two claimants join together to provide the requisite water.

When the heat of June bore down on the desert, my grandmother decided to return to Iowa. Her improvement turned out to have been temporary. There was, she said, a doctor back in Waterloo who seemed to help her, and she wanted to consult him again.

Father wired his brother Graham, asking if he could come at once. Graham responded, and a week later, he and his mother were on a train traveling eastward.

It was my grandmother's last trip. They had scarcely crossed the territorial line into New Mexico when the end came. She died in her son's arms. Her body was removed at Deming and buried there, as she could not be taken home. The news of her death was a severe blow to my father, as well as my mother. The family bonds had been very close. A time for tears had come.

That he had done the right thing in acquiring additional land Mother did not let Father doubt. The acquisition would stabilize their base of operations. She knew as well as Father that the road ahead of them was full of ruts and rocks. They would meet them as they came.

Father worked at the new project whenever he could spare a few hours from his other ranch duties. He did not neglect his potato project. He chose a quarter-acre site at the northeast corner of his timber claim, fenced it, and commenced the digging of a well. Digging a few feet at a time, he soon reached a point where it was as deep as he could go without installing hoisting equipment. In preparation for this, he built a platform around the excavation and the first few feet of curbing. Then he placed ditches along the north and south lines of the timber claims, which would serve notice that the work of proving up had begun. Already he noted curiosity on Snider's part as to what he might be planning to do on that waterless ground. Father had seen him ride by and watch his work from a clump of trees.

With this done, he could turn to other important things. He concentrated on the business of raising potatoes and increasing the number of his cattle. During the following few years he saw his herd grow to a hundred animals, then climb toward the two hundred mark. He had to hire help at branding time. Each year he was able to drive steers to market, but increasing commitments kept him spare of cash, and he continued to clear more land.

One evening in 1889, there appeared at the ranch a blond young man, coming afoot, seemingly out of nowhere. He carried a carpetbag slung over his shoulder. Near the front door was a rawhide-bottomed chair into which he sank. He took off a battered felt hat and wiped his forehead.

"Whew!" he said. "That walk from Phoenix was a long one."

Father didn't recognize the new arrival.

"Is there anything I can do for you?"

"I just came for a visit." His face broke into a grin.

Father pondered for a little while, combing his beard with his fingers. This was puzzling.

"Is supper ready?" the grinning man asked.

Then suddenly, Father knew. Well, two could play at that game.

"I think," he said, "we might spare you a plate of beans. Come this way."

He led the newcomer around the house and out to the woodpile. He pointed to the chopping block, the axe, and a pile of wood.

"Go to it," he said. "Come in at dark and we'll give you something, though we don't usually feed tramps."

The grin had gone from the visitor's face.

"Aw, now, Frank," he said. "I was just joking. I'm Lyssie."

"Lyssie?" Father scratched his head. "Should I know you? That sounds like a girl's name. Lyssie? Melissa?" It was Father who was grinning now.

"We Youngs gotta' have our jokes," the visitor said, holding out his hand. "I'm Ulysses Grant Young, as I think you know, Cousin Frank."

Laughing, they shook hands, and Frank took the new arrival into the house for introductions.

Lyssie—so called by all—was a second cousin, their grandfathers having been brothers. His family had settled in Kansas, and he had grown up there. But he didn't like the flat country, and like his ancestors, kept moving west.

He was made welcome, and was eager to help, even after having been warned by Father that he might not be able to give him steady work. Lyssie didn't mind. Responsibility did not weigh heavily upon him. He was light-hearted and something of a joker, as the manner of his arrival portended. He said he would stick around for awhile. Father's stock-raising included the breeding of some good horses, and as Lyssie seemed to be good with horses, he could help in the breaking of the young stock. As the herd of cattle increased they needed more and more attention and Lyssie could also help with that.

As it turned out, he was with us for a number of years, except for a break when he was given charge of a stage station at Harqua Hala, down by Yuma. The stage line went broke and Lyssie found he had been working for nothing except food and a cot.

The clearing of land went on, especially during the winter seasons, and finally all of the bottom land was clean. Because of some irregularities in the land level as the clearing approached the river, Father bought a horse-drawn wheel grader, and all the irrigable land was leveled out, ditched, and cross-fenced. In addition to the land reserved for potatoes and an acre or two for garden crops, Father had eighty acres in alfalfa, which grew so vigorously that he could cut five crops of hay, and sometimes six, in one season. The hay stacks near the corrals grew wider and wider, taller and taller, an excellent store of winter feed for the livestock.

With the continuing expansion of his potato plantings, Father found the need for a faster method of harvesting the crops than by spade or fork. He used a considerable part of one cattle sale to buy equipment, the main pieces being a planter and digger; the latter required four horses to power it. It was a good investment, saving a great deal of labor.

Father and Mother continued to plan for a new home during these busy years. A site was selected closer to the eastern boundary of the homestead, leaving room in front for shade trees and flowers. At one side would be a driveway. Father found time to plow ditches on either side of the proposed route and plant a row of fig trees on one side and pomegranates on the other. The site staked out for a well was close to the house-to-be.

"We'll have a pump and windmill," Father said, "and water piped to the kitchen and bathroom."

"What a wonderful thing that will be," Mother said wistfully.

Construction at the new homesite was actually started when Father found he needed storage space for potatoes until they could be marketed. With a plow, a scraper, and the help of Chappo and Lyssie, he excavated what was to be the cellar of the new house, then covered it with a frame of cottonwood poles and a heavy thatch of watermoties and straw. This provided a fairly cool storage space for the potato crop.

The time for gaining title to his homestead was at hand; he had met all requirements, but there was still the timber claim to worry about. He must get water on the land. He spent a winter with Lyssie and Chappo on the well. The land had greater elevation than at the homesite, and they had to dig fifty feet before they found a good flow of water. My father used redwood timbering, which was more expensive than pine but much more resistant to rot. A sturdy ladder was attached to the curbing as digging advanced. A windlass, rope, and heavy bucket were the means for hoisting excavated material. By hard work they could dig several feet a day.

Now the most important problem of all remained—getting the water to the surface, in quantity to be of practical use. There was only one solution: a steam-powered pump, which meant not only a centrifugal pump, but a boiler and engine to operate it. Was this possible, or were his hopes and dreams in vain?

He consulted a salesman for a firm that sold farm and industrial machinery, and they worked out the type of equipment that would be needed for a fifty foot well. The cost was appalling. How could he raise it?

Father consulted his banker, who stated that the bank could not help, but perhaps a loan agency operated by Henry Robinson could. Would the bank consider a mortgage? What on? He did not yet have the papers from Washington certifying title to the homestead acreage. Finally, Father saw Robinson; he agreed to loan half the purchase price of the pumping equipment if Father would put up the other half.

That summer he harvested a better-than-usual potato crop. He had more money in the bank than he had ever had. He drove more cattle to market than he should have driven. But, by borrowing on a two-year note, he raised enough money to take the biggest gamble of his life. The steam-operated pumping plant was ordered.

That winter, the pump was installed and the boiler and engine mounted. The great start-up took place on a warm spring day. The boiler was filled with water, the firebox crammed with wood. It was a Saturday, and everyone living on the ranch was there. My mother sat on the wagon seat, the silk umbrella she had brought from Ohio shielding her from the sun.

The fire was lit, smoke poured enchantingly from the smoke stack, and soon one could hear the hissing of escaping steam. Father manipulated various valves, and the piston of the engine began to move up and down. Father pulled a lever that engaged a clutch, and a pulley began to turn. The belt activated by this pulley sank out of sight in the depths of the well, where it started the centrifugal pump. Lyssie was down there seeing that the pump was properly primed. A tube ran from the pump to the surface, where it was bent to discharge into a box at the head of a ditch.

We waited anxiously for the water to appear. We waited and waited. A look of worry began to appear on Father's face. He looked at the steam gauge.

"Too low," he muttered. He pushed Chappo aside and began stoking furiously. He made certain that the back of the firebox was crammed with burning wood as well as the front. The steam pressure began to rise. What made the water so slow in coming?

He looked at the steam gauge again. It was near the safety-valve blow point. Could it be that all the planning, toil, sweat, worry, and money had been spent to no avail?

Suddenly cries came from the well.

"It's come, Frank!" Mother called.

And so it had. A stream of clear water spurted from the tube and began running down the ditch.

Smiling, Father took Mother and the children home, then returned to the well. A feeling of intense relief, of buoyancy, replaced the sinking feeling that almost became despair when the water failed to come.

Cottonwood limbs were trimmed and planted along the ditches. These would sprout and become trees if kept watered. The principal requirement of his contract with the government had now been fulfilled.

Some of the most strenuous years of the family's desert life were on the horizon. The depression of the early nineties spread its tentacles into Arizona. The price and demand for beef cattle fell, and at times there was no market at all. And for the first time, Father had no market for an entire potato crop. He found himself feeding potatoes to his cattle.

Then the worst blow of Father's and Mother's ranching career struck.

When the two-year note for the pump loan was about to become due, Father went to Robinson and asked for an extension. Robinson would not give it to him.

"Just go on paying the interest and I'll let it ride," he promised.

Father was tending a young orchard he had planted near the house when he saw Lawrence approaching at a furious gallop. He and Lyssie were watching the herd that day. I was there to hear Lawrence tell of a happening that Father had devoutly hoped might never occur.

"Papa!" Lawrence was so excited he got out the words with difficulty. "They're tearing down the pump—they're loading it on wagons."

"Saddle my horse!" he commanded Lawrence. He rushed into the house and seized his rifle. He quickly told Mother of the outrage that was being perpetrated.

"Robinson lied to me!" Father shouted. "He promised he'd give me time. I cannot stand for this."

He started away, Mother clinging to his arm and crying, "No, Frank, no! Please don't!"

I watched, frightened. Father was normally a man of mild temper, seldom showing annoyance, much less giving way to anger. True, I had seen him angry with me over some of my less trivial provocations, but it was anger well controlled, and he never whipped me while in that mood. Punishment came only after due consideration.

But on this occasion I saw my father in a fit of blazing fury over a man's broken promise, over what he believed to be a blasted hope built on great hardship and sacrifice, over money spent in an amount easily sufficient to build the comfortable home he and Mother had so long hoped and planned for.

The very force of Father's anger frightened me. I was only seven, but I had been taught the Ten Commandments; "Thou shalt not kill" flashed into my mind. I was relieved to see Mother's pleading finally prevail.

Father put away his rifle, and told Lawrence to unsaddle his horse. He would not go up to the well to be tortured by the totality of his defeat.

It took him a long time to get over the hurt left by that affair. Eventually, it was alleviated by the fact that his earnest effort to conform to the rules covering timber claims, his large expenditure, and his actually pumping water and planting trees entitled him to the patents for the two tracts that he eventually received. But he did not anticipate this on the dark day his pumping plant was hauled away. For the rest of the day, he remained at the house, too sick in his soul to think of the work awaiting him.

Father had been taught scrupulous honesty. "A man's word is his bond" was a principle that had been instilled into him. He believed it applied especially on the frontier, where lawyers and notaries public and legal forms might be hard to find. Even worse, he felt he had let his family down. He had spent money and weeks of toil that should have been expended for the comfort of his wife and children.

Mother would not join Father in his gloom. Her cheerful treatment of the tragedy, as though it was only a trifling incident in the life of a family on its way to better things, and her sympathy lifted his thoughts out of the darkness of his despondency.

That night he earnestly prayed that he might be forgiven for evil thoughts. He prayed that the man who wronged him might be forgiven. He thanked God for the love and support of his family. The next day, he was his calm self again, engaged in the problems of raising and marketing cattle and potatoes.

Father was not, however, to have seen the last of well digging. It was a well that came close to causing a tragedy. For months to come, the memory of this close call chilled the blood of all of us old enough to understand.

There never seemed time enough to do what had to be done, Father often remarked. Dawn to dark, six days a week. Sunday was a day of leisure, when it could be managed, but that was not always possible.

Mother paid no attention to a daylight schedule. Until Fay and I were old enough to take a hand, she managed by herself the multitude of household chores that are a part of rural life everywhere. And it was harder in pioneering days when there were so few conveniences. All washing, and there was a lot of it, was done with washboard and tub; ironing, by a flat iron heated on the stove. Mother made most of the children's clothes. By sewing up rips and patching holes, she made them last a long time. Her little foot-powered sewing machine really got a workout.

She kept us supplied with good homemade bread, biscuits, pan bread, and cakes and pies as she could manage. We loved our Sunday morning breakfasts of pancakes, ham, fried potatoes, and brown sugar syrup.

After a hard day's work, whether in fact or by pretense, she always appeared to be less tired than Father. She even offered to do some of the outside chores, such as milking, which she learned to do on her father's farm. But Father set his foot down at that. He tried to do such tasks as drawing the water himself, but she often went to the well anyhow. It was Mother who made the last trip to that well, with frightening consequences.

The Arizona desert country is a dry land, "the land of little rain." Yet it has its wet years. Following periods of drought, perhaps as long as ten years (or more or less), I have seen the normally dry Agua Fria and New River running streams almost continuously from October to May.

One evening, on a rainy day in early spring, Father came in, wet to the skin, and quickly began changing into dry clothing. What a great season this would be, he was thinking. The ground was already saturated down well over a foot, and would hold some of the water for months. This would be a year for deep-rooted lilies to bloom. The whole desert would be ablaze with color. He would load his family into a wagon and they would explore and search for rare flowers.

His reverie was suddenly interrupted. He heard his name called, frantically. It sounded like Mother's voice. He hurried into the back room. Mother was not there, but he heard the call again. Now it seemed to come from outside the house.

Lawrence had heard the first call and had gone to investigate. Now he came rushing up to Father, his face fear-stricken.

"Mother's down the well!" he yelled.

Father rushed over, finding to his horror that one of the uncurbed walls had caved in, plunging a side of the flimsy covering into the well. On the caved side, the platform had jammed, leaving it with one edge at the surface, the other a dozen feet down at a deep slant. The uprights that supported the cross-beam with the pulley had been torn away, wrecking the box that surrounded the opening. Mother was down there, clinging to the lower edge of the platform, her legs dangling over the deep pit.

If Mother loosed her hold, she would drop into the pit. Earth could still be heard falling in great amounts. She might be buried if she weakened and dropped into the gaping maw of the well.

"Hang on!" Father shouted. He thought of a rope. There was none at the house. He dispatched Lawrence to find one, fast. Then he thought of the twelve-foot ladder he kept at the rear of the house. Quickly, he carried it to the well and slid it down the steeply sloping side of the fallen platform until its lower rung was close to mother's hands.

"Can you grab ahold?" he called.

She had the strength. Slowly, Father lifted the ladder with its precious clinging burden until it was high enough to grasp her in his arms.

Mother cried a little, then angrily brushed the tears away.

"What am I doing that for?" she asked. Then added, "That was an exciting trip, but I don't want to repeat it. Come on, children, and help me finish supper."

We had been watching in fascinated fright, but Mother's quick recovery helped calm us.

We were without well water for awhile. Father made eave troughs to catch rain water, but most of what we used was hauled in barrels from the canal. Then, as it was still high-water time in the rivers, we had to let the mud settle out and boil what was to be used for food and drink.

It was a month before Father managed to get a new well dug, up where the new house was to be built. It was well-curbed, one may be sure. But its water was raised by rope, pulley, and bucket. No pump, no windmill. We who had the privilege of supplying the house now had to pack it down in pails and cans for a hundred yards.

CHAPTER 6

Then We Were Seven

IN THE SPRING OF 1890, WHEN IT BECAME CLEAR THAT mother was to have a fourth child, Father arranged to send her and his three children to Ohio to escape the worst of the summer heat. It was an event on that trip that implanted my first conscious memory.

We were visiting at Graham Villa, the house of Uncle Olie and Aunt Emma, who was Mother's sister. They had a son older than I who had a little wagon, which I coveted. My instincts at less than three years were completely primal, and I determined to possess that little vehicle by any means possible, even to engaging in combat—which I proceeded to do.

When Aunt Emma's keen ears picked up sounds which she correctly interpreted as the furor of battle, she charged to the scene and appropriated the wagon, leaving us nothing to fight over. The scolding she gave us was expressed in such lucid and eloquent verbiage that it was burned into my memory as with a branding iron.

I have one more clear memory originating in that year. It was in November, after my third birthday. It was early morning, before dawn had broken. I was sleeping soundly on my cot in the back room when I was startled by a sound which turned my bones to water—a wailing cry, rising and falling in crescendo. I finally placed it as coming from the front room, far away from my cot. Around the edges of the curtain that hung in the doorway between the two rooms, I could see light, and could imagine my father having arisen from his bed to do battle with some dreadful thing from the night. When the first wave of my paralyzing fear had passed, I found my voice.

"Papa!" I yelled. When I heard no answer, I yelled again, and waited. Had the thing got him? Was I to be next?

I had just pulled my blanket over my head and curled up in a ball, all I could do to ward off the terrible fate that must be awaiting me, when the blanket was jerked off. Father stood beside my cot, a lamp in his hand.

"I heard you calling," he said. "Anything the matter?"

"I heard something awful . . ." I choked up.

Father laughed. "That 'awful' thing is a new baby sister," he said, "cute as can be. Mama and I are both all right. Go to sleep now."

Thus did my sister Virna arrive, and thus was that night burned deep into my slowly evolving memory.

When Vivian came along two years later, I was old enough not to be frightened at an infant's wail. This event occurred on a cloudy afternoon in August. While Father, an expert in the delivery of babies by now, was attending Mother, Lyssie took us children on a long walk. By the time we returned, Vivian had arrived.

This was the last such event my father was to have the pleasure of presiding over.

From that time on, my memory of important happenings on the ranch is keen, perhaps because there was no clutter of happenings to lessen their impact such as there is in the city.

As soon as I was able to function, I was assigned to keep the wood box filled, and a pail of kindling chips from the wood pile at hand. In addition to the mesquite fuel, a pile of driftwood from the river bottom was always to be available. This being mostly soft cottonwood, its mixture with the mesquite and catclaw hardwood could fuel a hot stove in little time. There was a galling mixture of other chores as time went on—gathering eggs, feeding chickens, watering the work horses and graining them, milking, and whatever else came to hand. The other children had their assignments. These were mainly indoor tasks, except for Lawrence.

My brother, three and a half years older than I, was a steady lad, lacking my propensity for indolence and dreams. He was well aware of his status as the older son; at an early age, as soon as he had acquired the necessary riding skill, he was of real help with the herd. At the same time, he explored the three R's under Mother's tutelage.

Fay was trained early in the ways of the housekeeper, and became Mother's first assistant as the years advanced.

Father, well realizing that his children's attendance at school must be by horseback transportation, taught us to ride at the earliest possible age. We boys were riding at six. At eight, I had my own pony and rode with full confidence that my feet would come out of the stirrups only as I myself should will.

My sister Fay also became a good rider, and the younger girls came to yearn for the time when they, too, could join the cavalry. In those days, members of the feminine sex were not supposed to allow any part of the lower extremities to be visible below the ankles; wearing pants would be the ultimate horror. Females would dare to mount a horse only upon a side saddle and only wearing a long riding skirt. Fay was thus equipped when first she rode to school.

I was probably not older than my fourth year when I first found myself atop a horse, but I remember that event clearly enough. Father had a big gray stallion he had named Tiglath Pelezer, after a fabled Assyrian king. He was, of course, known as Tig. He was gentle, and to give me the feel of a horse's back, Father lifted me up and sat me down. My legs were too short to be of any use in holding on, but I did manage to get hold of the short end of the stallion's mane. Father went to Tig's head, intending to lead him a few steps to give me a sense of movement.

"Hang on tight, now," he cautioned.

I looked down, which I should not have done. The ground seemed far off, as far as from the top of the house. A feeling of dizziness swept over me and I began to slide down Tig's sleek side.

"Papa!" I screamed. "I'm . . ." But before Father could reach me, I dived head first to the ground.

When I woke up, I was on my cot in the house and Mother was placing cold packs on my aching head. Father stood by, a worried look on his face.

"I should have watched closer," he declared. Fearing my experience might engender a fear of horses, Father saddled up Tig next day and placed me behind the cantle, to which I clung for dear life. We took a slow ride around the yard, and I soon found myself enjoying the experience.

The West End School was three and a half miles away. Each of us, under Mother's tutelage, was able to join the third-year classes when we began attendance in our eighth years. She was a good teacher, and had concentrated on reading as the base for all other learning, though she had not neglected "writin' and 'rithmetic."

Father turned over a box of young people's reading matter saved from his own boyhood to Lawrence and me. Included were a stack of copies of a boys' magazine, in which I found a plethora of foods for my dreamings. My favorite reading was of serialized stories by Oliver Optic, perhaps the best-known writer of juvenile fiction of the period. Especially fascinating were a group of adventures in sail boats on a large lake. After reading them, I knew my aim in life had been settled. I would be a sailor. And I must start my training at once—a difficult thing to do as the largest body of water I had ever seen was the half-acre tank my father had constructed when the expansion of his herd called for it.

I was about eight at the time. I asked Father to get me a boat. That, he said, was out of the question. He kindly suggested I build a raft of some of the railroad ties we had rescued from the river at flood time. I could use them if I didn't let my project interfere with my work. So I dragged half a dozen ties to the edge of my lake, laid them side by side, and nailed scraps of battens crosswise to hold them together.

Lawrence had come over to watch the goings on at my shipyard.

"Better put in more nails," he advised. "Looks pretty rickety."

I paid him no mind. I saw some dark clouds on the horizon, and I wanted to put to sea in fair weather. I nailed uprights for masts on either side, and used an old piece of canvas for a sail.

"What do you call her?" Lawrence asked.

"The *Pirate*."

"Better change that to Hesperus," he said. "Looks like it's going to go to pieces." We had heard Longfellow's poem recited at school.

He helped me slide my ship into the water.

"I'll take one passenger," I invited. "Get on."

"You're crazy," Lawrence jeered. "I'd sink it. You'll ride alone. I'll stay on shore and watch the shipwreck."

The pond was maybe fifty yards across, farther if a diagonal course were taken. I decided to go that way, and a southwest wind, getting stronger by the minute, would help me. I had a pole to steer with. A blast of wind smelling of rain struck the sail, causing the front of my ship to submerge. I had to stand at the stern to keep it level.

Away we went, my heart pounding with joy over the voyage that I was certain would be the first of many on the bounding main, as the books called the ocean. All around me, little waves were breaking into white froth. Foam from the bow of my charging ship was carried by the wind.

The first, and last, voyage of the *Pirate* under sail lasted less than a minute. It did some unnecessary tacking, and at the end of the journey, the ship, instead of pursuing a straight northeast course, veered north-northeast and hit the shore line at an angle.

The timber on the port side was the first to strike and was torn away from the rest of the craft. The same thing happened to the other "beams" in rapid succession.

The skipper of the *Pirate* floundered in the water among the wreckage. Lawrence pulled me out. He laughed and laughed. "You can name this spot the reef at Norman's Woe," he giggled. Lawrence told of my voyage at supper that night. Everyone but me thought it was very funny.

"You just wait," I said. "I'll show you!"

But reviewing the situation on my cot that night, I thought maybe I wouldn't be a sailor after all. Maybe I'd just travel around the world and write books. I dreamed of new triumphs. My mind wandered back to the first story I had written, a year or two before.

For a long time, I had noticed a reflection on some shining object off to the west during sunny afternoons, apparently near the White Tank hills.

"What is it?" I asked Father. He had seen it, too.

"It may be the sun shining on a piece of tin, like from a coal oil can. Maybe a prospector has built a cabin and used flattened-out coal oil cans for a roof."

As I pondered on this, another idea occurred to me. Maybe that shining thing wasn't tin. What if it was gold the prospectors hadn't found? It was a breath-taking thought.

That would make a good story. I found a tablet and pencil and went to work. I knew Father and Mother needed money, as I had heard them say they'd have to wait a little longer for the new house. That motivated the trend of my masterpiece-to-be, which went about like this:

John and Mary's papa and mama went to town and left them on the ranch alone.

"Papa and Mama are worried," John said. "What is the matter?"

"They need money," Mary said.

"I wish we could find some," John said.

"How?" Mary said.

"Maybe there is gold in the mountains. Something is shining over there."

"Let us look," said Mary.

So they saddled their ponies and after riding all morning they found the shining thing and it was a chunk of gold so big it was hard to carry and when they got home their papa and mama were already there and when they started to scold them for leaving the ranch they gave them the gold and they forgot about scolding and Papa said, "Bless you, my children," and he took the gold and paid all they owed and they were all happy for a long time.

Father was reading a newspaper that evening, and Mother was darning socks when, the glow of accomplishment still on me, I dared break the news to them.

"I wrote a story," I announced.

Father read the story aloud, and they both praised the fine work, hugged me, and thanked me for wanting to help.

In teaching their children how to address them, my parents had chosen to be called "Papa" and "Mama," which in polite circles, in their domain at least, was the custom of the period. "Father" and "Mother" were considered to be too formal, not intimate enough for the affectionate relationship that should prevail between parents and children. "Pa" and "Ma" were too plebian, and in those days "Dad" and "Mom" were unknown.

My parents were also concerned about the purity of the language we used. They sought diligently to discourage the use of bad grammar and vulgarisms learned from our contact with the herd men. I wasn't very old when I brought to the house and, in ignorance, used some words so shocking that Mother nearly fainted. From Father, I was given a crash course in the proper use of the language and the necessity of avoiding lingual indecencies. Never, I was commanded, utter a word you do not understand.

Father was not without the use of an expletive when aggravated. If he used this when any of his children were near, he would say, "No

one should ever display temper. I ask you not to follow my example."
This particular expletive was "Plague on it!"

After I had started school I brought home the expression, "Doggone it"; it was met with disfavor.

With the aid of Mother's foot-powered sewing machine, which she had brought from Ohio, she turned out many garments for her children, especially the girls. With many of the garments there was progression based on age, from one sibling to a younger one. There was real economy in this system, a factor of no interest to me when I began to feel the shame of wearing my sister Fay's dresses. I guess I was about five years old when I balked after the hired men began to call me "Annie." Then my mother cut a pattern and put me in pants.

The years slowly came and went. Still the new home was not built. Father continued to talk of starting it; Mother, to advise paying all debts first and building up a bank account.

How soon would that home come? Was it to be or not to be?

CHAPTER 7

Home at
Brushwood Manor

AS I GREW OLDER, AND AFTER AN OCCASIONAL TRIP TO town with my father, I began to note that most of the ranches had better houses than ours. But that fact didn't bother me in the least; the other ranchers had been there longer than we. Besides, we were to have a fine house, better than most of the others, I was sure.

Though our little house might be called a shack or a shanty, to the Frank Young family it was a real home, filled with love and warmth. It even acquired a fanciful name.

One cool evening in spring, after Father had been reading a story to us about some children who lived in a dwelling called a manor house, Mother said lightly:

"Perhaps we should dignify our little mansion by calling it Young Manor."

"Or Agua Fria Manor," Lawrence suggested.

"How about Greasewood Manor?" Fay chimed in.

Father laughed. "Some might think," he said, "that 'greasewood' lacks the poetic touch, though it is applicable. It is brush, and we have lots of that."

"Then would Brushwood Manor be poetic enough?" Mother asked.

We all agreed that sounded just fine, for, as Father mentioned, there was lots of brush around, even on top of our shade. We should have an appropriate display of our new name, I thought. Next day, I found a discarded three-foot strip of batt, sneaked out a bottle of ink from among the writing materials on a shelf of the whatnot, made a brush by wrapping a strip of cloth around the edge of a twig, and lettered "Brushwood Manner" on the strip. Then, when no one was in the house, I tacked it over the front door.

I heard my parents laughing when they discovered it, but they offered me no praise. Lawrence jeered:

"Don't you know how to spell?"

My feeling of pride evaporated. After a few days, the sign I had so carefully lettered disappeared.

As limited as our living accommodations were, our parents endeavored to give us as good a life as circumstances permitted. They were concerned that the memory of the rather stark conditions we were forced to contend with would, in later life, engender a feeling that they had let us down. They need not have worried. Their love and intimate concern for the development of our minds and bodies overshadowed any discomforts, for such as there were we simply accepted as a necessary part of what we then and since considered to be a normal life with a good share of happiness.

When Father felt he could, he would bring to the house new things designed to add comfort to family living. Once he brought Mother a new rocking chair, at other times new dishes and cutlery—things that would be a credit to the new home. He bought Lawrence a twenty-two caliber single shot rifle. He saw that the children had things that would be useful as well as give pleasure, such as the wagon which was large enough to haul firewood and water from the well.

Coming from town late one summer evening after a good potato crop had been harvested, he drove up to the front of the house. In the bed of the wagon was a large wooden crate. He called for Lyssie and Chappo to bring him a couple of planks and a claw hammer. Curious, all five children gathered around. Father's manner was mysterious and we anticipated something exciting.

The planks were placed at the rear of the wagon and the big box skidded down to the ground. It was getting dark. Lanterns were brought. Father pried off the front of the box. Still, we couldn't see what was there, as heavy paper covered whatever rested inside. Father took his knife, cut down the sides of the paper and all but a small strip at the top. He took hold of the edge.

"Hurry up, Papa!" I implored.

Father sent a reproving look upon me, and I shrank back.

"This," he said, "is for all of us, but especially," he bowed toward Mother, "the queen of the castle."

He turned, grasped the top of the paper with both hands, and ripped it down and away.

A lovely, shining organ showed its polished face to us.

Father unfastened the stool tied beneath the bank of keys while we children shouted our pleasure and Lyssie and Chappo stood grinning. Father seated Mother on the stool.

"Play, your highness," he commanded.

Mother was no stranger to the organ, as her training had included music lessons. She tried a few tentative chords, then began to play "Lead, Kindly Light," which she knew to be Father's favorite hymn. With her sweet soprano voice she sang, and Father joined in with his bass.

Unnoticed at first, the forms of several men from the harvesting gang had gathered at the edge of the circle of lantern light. As Mother finished the hymn we were surprised to hear shouts of "Ole!" a clapping of hands, and "More, more!" They had been lured by the beautiful and unexpected music.

Mother played some popular songs, and Father invited the men to join in. Two or three did: There was a clear and melodious voice among them. Father told him to come forward. Side by side they sang, the bass and tenor and soprano blending well together with the entrancing organ tones.

Mother ended the concert by playing "Battle Hymn of the Republic," its lively pace stirring our blood and bringing lumps to our throats. It was the best evening we had ever experienced.

Always, before bedtime, Father conducted a devotional period. That night, for the first time, we had musical accompaniment to the closing hymn.

Our daily routine reflected my parents' religious upbringing. Their center of life outside the family circle had been the church. On the ranch, a devotional period was set aside both morning and night. At the table before all meals Father asked "the blessing"; after breakfast we had Bible reading, prayer, and a verse of song. Hired hands, who sat with the family at a common table, were invited to join the brief services, but we were almost always alone. We were all taught a bed-side prayer as soon as we were able to talk.

Though it must have been hard at times, Father and Mother strove always to maintain a cheerful front. They often used mealtime to bring back into balance attitudes among the siblings that might have been disturbed. My father had a horde of amusing anecdotes, and he was expert at chasing gloom by narrating them. Now and then he would find in a story a little lesson for his children.

These stories were supplemented by such reading materials as our parents felt would give us pleasure and also, when possible, be infor-mative. There were children's books from the kindergarten type to the advanced grades, and how eagerly we looked forward to the weekly *Youth's Companion!* Its stories and articles were entrancing! Father subscribed to magazines on farming, bee culture, science, and current events. Mother had her *Christian Herald* and *The Mayflower,* a magazine for the flower lover. It was in *The Mayflower* that Mother found articles by Sharlot Hall relating to native flora in the area where she lived, which helped in our family's study of desert growth. In later years, Sharlot Hall became famous throughout the Southwest for her stirring poetry. After Arizona achieved statehood she was known as its poet laureate, historian, and librarian.

In addition to our adventures through books, we had ample room for outdoor entertainment, and on special occasions, travel.

A few rods from the house was a large mesquite tree, standing on the upper part of the homestead. When Father first came, he found it of use as a chicken roost and as a makeshift shelter for the horses. Later, he built a combined chicken house and harness room, and open sheds and manger for the horses. The harness room also held a work bench with tools and space for cots for a few hired men. Now the big tree was available as a play room for the children. Father hung a swing and built a teeter-totter and merry-go-round close by.

As we grew older, each of us was given a chance to visit the city, that we might learn what the larger world was like. My first excursion took place when I was six. Father took me with him on one of his weekly trips, and I goggled in amazement at the great buildings tower-ing into the sky, many as high as two stories, a few of three!

The horse and buggy are stopped in the center of the dirt thoroughfare that passed in front of the Hotel Adams, right. Date unknown. Courtesy, Arizona Department of Library, Archives and Public Records

"I guess this is the biggest town in the world," I informed my father.

"Hardly," said Father. "But it's growing fast—twenty years ago it was only a little village. Now it has about thirty-five hundred citizens."

We went to a restaurant for lunch. We were waited on by a man with a braid of black hair hanging down his back. I ate some pie that wasn't nearly as good as Mother's, and the first ice cream I had ever tasted. It was so cold it made my head ache something awful. It was a thoroughly exciting experience, nonetheless.

The most anxiously anticipated holiday of the year was, of course, Christmas.

Christmastime in the desert, as everywhere, was an event awaited with intense eagerness. While we children never received such an outpouring of gifts as youngsters expect nowadays, we could always count on getting something we had longed for, whether a book, a dress, a wheeled toy, or a doll. When Father had got me a pony and saddle, behind my pleasure was the feeling that I could never be a real cowboy until I had a lasso like the other riders on the ranch. At various times and in various ways I attempted to impress this fact on my father, but he never seemed to give the matter a thought, vital as it was. When Christmas arrived that year I found no lasso beneath my stocking. I tried not to show my disappointment, and tried to be happy with what I did get.

When Father had finished distributing the gifts too large for the stockings, he said:

"Though we live on the frontier and have to endure many inconveniences at times, all pioneers have had the same troubles. Your grandparents had things that way in their young days in Ohio, way back before the Civil War. My mother told me that one Christmas when she was a child all she found in her stocking were one red apple and a bright copper penny."

He went outside, Lawrence with him. A little later my brother returned.

"Papa wants you to go out to the swing," he said. "Hurry."

I went out and began to run toward the big mesquite. Suddenly I heard a swishing sound in my ear, and a loop settled over my head and shoulders, pinioning my arms. I began to be pulled backwards. I yelled.

I heard Father laughing. I turned my head and saw him pulling me toward him, hand over hand. He released me, coiled up the lasso, and handed it to me.

"More Merry Christmas," he said.

In a state of thrilled delight, I ran to the harness room and tied the loop to my saddle beside the horn. I stepped back and stood for several minutes admiring that beautiful length of coiled rope. Now I could join that favored group, riders with lassoes. I had received my patent of nobility.

CHAPTER 8

Buttermilk Biscuits
and Jerky Gravy

ONCE, WHEN I WAS DESCRIBING TO A FRIEND SOME OF THE
phases of life on a desert homestead, he asked:

"What in the world did you find to eat in a barren place like that?"

He looked skeptical when I told him we fared as well and possibly
better than city dwellers.

Most of the time we had a good variety of food gathered from the
ranch or close about. We had our own vegetables and fruits in season,
and there was always meat in abundant variety.

Father brought with him not only his forty-four caliber Colt repeating rifle and ten gauge double-barreled shotgun but cartridge loading
equipment as well. For the shotgun he used brass shells, loaded as
used, mostly with bird shot but a few with buckshot. When I became
old enough, Father would let me help punch out spent caps, press in
fresh ones with the tool made for that purpose, then press in the wads
after the measured powder and pour in the shot loads. For rifle car-
tridges, he had a small bullet mould and a bar of lead. He melted the
lead in a small ladle over mesquite coals.

There was never a dearth of small game. Cottontail rabbits, fat
from eating desert plants and grasses or alfalfa from Father's fields,

were mighty good eating, rivaling chicken in excellence. There were the quail, the most plentiful of all birds. I have already related how they invaded newly planted grain fields, coming in off the range by the hundreds. Over the years Father managed to accommodate himself to them. By harrowing the seed deep, he was able to raise enough wheat for our poultry, even though, scratching like chickens, the quail got a fair share of it.

Father didn't believe in killing needlessly, but the quail at times were a real menace, not only to grain crops, but to young vegetables as well. There wasn't time to maintain a shotgun patrol, though many birds were indeed shot. Father devised traps, and baiting them with wheat, caught hundreds. Those that we couldn't eat were sold to restaurants in Phoenix.

Another benefit we got from quail was their eggs. Their preferred nesting spots were on the ground in thick growths of underbrush. There were such spots on the timber claim land close to our homestead ground, and we kids sometimes searched this area in nesting season, rejoicing when we could bring home two or three dozen fresh quail eggs. Fried or scrambled, they were a real treat.

Quail thus formed an important part of our diet. There were also other game birds native to the desert such as mourning doves and the larger white-wings, but they could not compare with quail for the table and were of small menace to crops, so they were pretty well let alone on our ranch.

Now and then we would have wild duck when a flock, or sometimes a loner, would settle on our larger stock tank. In fact, my first encounter with a shotgun occurred one morning when I saw a lone duck swimming in the big stock tank. Lawrence and Fay were in school, Father and Lyssie were with the herd, Chappo was irrigating, so I was temporarily the man of the house, left to look after Mother and the younger girls. When I saw the duck, I felt it was up to me to do something about it. I didn't consult Mother, though, out under the shade doing our laundry—after all, I was seven years old.

I slipped into the back room and lifted the big shotgun from its pegs. Taking two loaded shells out of the ammunition box and hurrying away, I slipped in the shells as I went. I knew all about guns. I had seen Father shoot his many times, and I had a proprietary interest in those ten-gauge shells, since I had helped load them.

The retaining bank of the tank was high enough to give me concealment as I crawled through the corral fence toward it. I raised up and peered cautiously over. The duck was swimming near the far bank.

I rested the gun on a strand of barbed wire. I had never been able to understand why a gun with two barrels had only the one sight between the barrels near the muzzles. That was a poor way to economize. Each barrel should have a sight. Well, I'd have to do the best I could in the face of such stupidity! Cocking the left barrel of the gun, I put the butt-plate to my shoulder—too loosely, I learned—sighted down the left barrel, and pulled the trigger.

Meantime, Mother wanted the wood box at the stove refilled, and called to me. When I didn't answer she asked Virna if she had seen me. Virna pointed toward the corrals, and said I went thataway, with a big gun. Sure enough, she found the shotgun was gone.

She hurried toward the corrals. As she came in sight of the tank, she saw me with the big gun to my shoulder. Frantically, she called out.

The roar of that ten-gauge cannon drowned out her words. I was just struggling to my feet out of the corral dust into which the mule-like kick of the gun had thrown me when Mother ran up. I was staggering, my hand to my shoulder, which felt pulverized. Her alarm dissipated when it became apparent that a bruised shoulder was the only damage done me.

"I shot at a duck," I explained.

Mother flicked a brief glance toward the pond. So did I. Neither of us saw any duck. She picked up the gun, broke it, extracted the shells and put them in her apron pocket. She handed the gun to me.

"Carry it back," she said.

At the house I was put to work at the churn, a job I hated.

"Aren't you going to whip me?" I asked.

"I'll let Papa take care of you," she answered.

It was late morning before I had a chance to slip away again. I ran to the pond. How could I have missed that duck? That left barrel was pointed right at it. I circled the shore—and when I reached the eastern side, there, at the edge of the water and half concealed by growth of weeds, lay my duck—the bird for which I suffered so much.

Joyfully, I retrieved the bird. I knew how to dress foul, so I plucked and drew the webfoot and carried it to Mother just as she started to call me. The scolding I expected was halted when she saw the bird.

"Mercy!" was all she said. That word was as close to an expletive as Mother ever got. It could be used with any type of emotion. Anyhow, we had roast duck for supper that night.

Duck was an occasional treat, but as in all cattle country, beef was king. When meat was needed, Father would butcher a young steer, and then we would enjoy cuts that no one bothered to classify, but now would be called T-bone or porterhouse or club or filet mignon, and such common stuff as round steaks and rump roasts. Then, too, there were the soups and stews and chunky gravy.

Finally, the remaining meat was cured to make jerky. To accomplish this, the lean meat was cut into strips, the fat cut away, and the strips salted and hung on wires in the sun. If the weather was hot, it took only a day or two for the meat to dry so hard it crackled. Then it was packed in cheesecloth sacks and stored, to be used when fresh meat was not at hand.

Of great help in keeping foods from spoiling was a piece of equipment which Father made himself, called the cool box, or cooler. This box was made of lumber and was about four feet square and five feet high, with legs that held it a foot above the ground. The legs were placed in tomato cans filled with water to keep out the little house ants which seemed to be as prevalent on the desert as elsewhere. The door was a frame covered by two thicknesses of gunny sacking. Two five-gallon oil cans were placed on top. Each had a row of small holes punched along the lower edge on one side. When the cans were filled, the water trickled down over the sacking, keeping it moist. Evaporation kept the interior of the box nice and cool. There were shelves for milk pans and a variety of perishable foods. The box was placed outdoors under the shade near the kitchen door. During the hottest months the stove was also moved outdoors.

I remember the cooler especially because it became my job to bring water from the well for the trickler cans. With the cooler's help we could manage to make butter through all but the hottest periods, though it could not be marketed during the hot periods. But we were not without butter fat at any season. Father was the one who introduced us to ghee, butter fat in a liquid state. It was made by "drying out" sour cream in a hot kettle, a process that separated the curds from the fat. It might congeal to some extent in the cooler, but if not, it could be served with a spoon.

An ice plant had been built in Phoenix, and in hot weather, on his weekly trips to the city, Father would bring home a hundred-pound block of ice. He would have the ice wrapped in a blanket, to my wonderment. Blankets were used to keep warm, so how could they keep ice cold? Father patiently explained this scientific mystery.

After that, the summer heat was made more bearable by iced lemonades and other cold drinks. Father got an ice cream freezer, an "if you turn the crank you get to lick the paddle" type. I still remember the ice cream Mother made. I would see her pour into the can rich whole milk supplemented by a pitcher of cream, fresh crushed peaches, sugar, and perhaps some spices.

A useful vessel always suspended beneath the shade with a dipper hanging at its side was the *olla* (oh-yah), Spanish for "hole." A pottery vessel made by Indians from clay and fired in a flame of mesquite, it was round with a flared mouth. Its use was to keep drinking water cool in hot weather, which it did efficiently, as the unglazed slow-fired clay left the vessel slightly porous. The water filtering through evaporated and had a cooling effect that left the water in the *olla* several degrees cooler than the outside atmosphere.

Though the *ollas* were sometimes hung in their bare state, more often they were wrapped in gunny sacking, which, when kept moist, further aided the cooling process. *Ollas* were made in various sizes; ours held perhaps two gallons of water. It was placed in a cradle of baling wire, then suspended from one of the poles that supported the thatch.

Father kept several milk cows, and my education in the art of extracting lacteal fluid from bovines began at six. A year later, I was assigned a gentle Jersey cow to milk, but until my hands grew stronger, Father did the finishing.

With plenty of skim milk available, Father decided to buy a pregnant sow. Soon, we had a pen full of little pigs. It wasn't long before we were able to add pork to our country fare.

Another familiar sight was a suspended cheese bag. Mother made delicious smearcase from clabbered milk. Placed in a cheesecloth bag, the whey drained away, leaving the curds in shape to be eaten.

One of the most important foods in the desert cuisine was the bean—the famed *frijole* (pronounced free-holy). No kitchen was without its bean pot on the stove. In preparing meals for a gang such as the ten or twelve men Father hired at harvest time, Mother relied on beans, the most important item on the table. The beans we ate at the ranch were of the old-fashioned pink variety. We would buy them in hundred-pound sacks, which cost in the neighborhood of two to three dollars. We never tired of beans as Mother cooked them, with pork or beef, onions, some molasses, and catsup. When the beans in the pot— the lower half of a five-gallon can—had been eaten for several meals and were of a thick consistency from repeated reheating, they would gain added flavor by being crisply fried, with more onions added.

When planting time came in early spring, Father would plant, in addition to his potatoes, several six hundred-foot rows of vegetables, enough so that even when quail and rabbits had made their forays, we would have plenty for our own table. During a season we might have green corn, turnips, beets, radishes, lettuce, squash, pumpkins, watermelons, muskmelons, peas, green beans, cabbage, and sweet potatoes.

The year after Father arrived, he planted a small orchard of peaches and apricots close to the house. Along the driveway leading to the proposed new house was a row of figs on one side and a row of pomegranates on the other. With our help, as we became old enough, Mother picked the fruits, canning some and sundrying apricots, peaches, and figs.

Potatoes, our spuds, were available to us most of the year, and Mother seemed to have inexhaustible ways to prepare them for the table. The harvesting was completed in June, and in August a second smaller crop would be planted. If the frost did not come unseasonably early, we could count on marketable spuds from this second crop. In any case, we would have eating potatoes through the winter. Little new potatoes in cream gravy were delicious. We had potatoes baked and boiled, fried and mashed, with cream, scalloped with ham, and in salad. Whenever it rained we had potato soup, and even on some cloudy days. To this day, stormy weather brings with it the memory of Mother's potato soup.

I still marvel at the variety and quantity of foods Mother could prepare on that little four-legged, four holer, wood burning stove. She could prepare a hot dinner for seven or seventeen. From the oven came pies, cakes, cookies, biscuits, and bread in what seemed an endless stream. How I loved to be served a heel from one of Mother's big, hot, round loaves with its delicious odor, drenched with butter and honey from Father's apiary.

One other dish that we all enjoyed was a combination of buttermilk biscuits and jerky gravy; it always brought praise from visitors and hired hands as well. Mother often fell back on dried beef when fresh meat was not at hand. Her special way of making this dish was to have the jerky pounded into flakes—my job—then, with flour slightly scorched, make a thick brown gravy and spoon it generously on large halved buttermilk biscuits.

Wild foods were scarce in the desert, but I should mention one of value to man and beast—the mesquite bean. These hung from the branches in golden clusters, their color rivaling the yellow blooms from which they sprang. This was great food for the cattle, who fattened on the luscious pods, sweet and tender if taken just after the color turns. We children also gained weight in mesquite bean season. Man's way of eating the beans is to chew the pods, extract the juice and what tender pulp may go with it, and eject the seeds and fiber. The aboriginal people made the mesquite bean a valuable part of their diet, grinding up the ripened beans into meal.

Finally, I can never forget those great big steaming pots of chicken and dumplings, country style, that my mother made. They were soul satisfying. First, you catch two fat, cornfed cockerels, and . . .

But everyone knows about chicken and dumplings.

Even though we did without a lot of life's comforts, we didn't fare so badly down Agua Fria way.

CHAPTER 9

Dangers in Desert Land

IN THE DAYS OF WHICH I WRITE, ARIZONA WAS A LAND OF mystery and terror to most people living east of the Rocky Mountains. It was thought to be a wild place of sand, cactus, blazing sun, murderous Indians and outlaws, and venomous reptiles and insects.

Before her arrival in Arizona and in spite of Father's soothing letters, Mother was not quite sure that the Apaches wouldn't invade the Salt River Valley, and that she would have to fight rattlesnakes every day. But after Geronimo surrendered the year of her arrival, she felt better, and she learned quickly to adapt herself to frontier life.

Though Father did not discount the hazards of frontier life, he took all reasonable precautions to meet them. He taught us the need for the avoidance of dangers as soon as we could comprehend, and he conveyed this part of our education by word and example.

In the desert the horse might often be the means to safety, and this fact far outweighed the infrequent danger from the horse itself. He put us in the saddle as soon as we could safely learn. The horse was the best means to get from one place to another, but he stressed that we should not take the horse and its equipment too casually, particularly when our duties took us out on the range.

"Inspect your equipment daily," he cautioned. "See that reins and cinches and latigos are sound. Never travel without a canteen of water, and don't forget the importance of a knife."

Before I became old enough to rate a jackknife of my own, Father was quite generous in loaning me his when he could watch to see I didn't cut myself. But one morning I failed to return his knife to him before he rode away. As a result, I was the recipient of an enlightening lecture on the evil of negligence, and how even such a small thing as a pocketknife might save a man's life in case he was set afoot in the desert, or bitten by a rattler.

Riding accidents were not numerous, but they did occur, such as that to a young man of a family known to us. One morning the father of the young man rode to our house.

"My son is missing," he told Father. "He was riding herd on our cattle. His horse came back, without the saddle. Will you help me hunt for him?"

"Surely," he said. "Here's a man who'll go along."

He called to Lyssie, who rode off with the anxious father.

The end of the search was a sad one. Guided by soaring buzzards, the searchers found the young man. His foot still in the stirrup that had held it while the horse dragged him to death, he lay in the desert brush.

"This should be a lesson to all of us," Father told Lawrence and me. "Such accidents have happened before. Men riding the range can prevent such accidents by wearing boots with high heels so the foot can't slip through the stirrup, or that are so loose around the ankle the foot can easily slip out."

As an added precaution, and also to protect the feet from thick brush and thorns, a common addition to the stirrup is the tapadero, a shield of heavy leather fastened to the front of the stirrup.

We didn't have boots, and Father didn't favor those of the high-heeled kind as they interfered with walking. We had a lot of that to do on the ranch. So Father gave us an added bit of advice.

"Whenever you ride," he said, "keep the laces on your shoes so loose your foot can slip out in case you're thrown."

Well, on the morning when I had one of the greatest frights of my life I must have forgotten what Father said.

It was a fine spring morning, the day that came so near to being the last I was to know. I was eight years old. Father was irrigating the orchard near the house, I was on my pony. Chappo came up.

"*Señor,*" he said to Father, "the cows, they get in the alfalfa."

"Herbert," Father called, "ride down and drive the cattle out of the alfalfa field, and see how they got in."

I liked horseback chores if they were short, so I galloped away, opening and closing the barbed wire gates that led to the field. Hay had been cut from it only a few days before, and already another growth had commenced. I then discovered that something was very wrong.

Cattle seem pretty smart at times. Some of them learned to open the gate by lifting the loop at the top of the five-foot pole that formed one end of the gate. This allowed the gate to drop down. That's what they had done here. The gate down, several cattle had walked through to eat the watery new alfalfa sprouts. This was enough to start them bloating. Their breathing labored, three of the animals were already suffering.

If these animals did not have prompt attention they would die, I knew. I put my pony into a hard gallop back to the orchard.

"Papa!" I yelled. "The cattle are . . ."

Those were my last words for some time. I had forgotten the clothesline stretched between two apricot trees. I almost reached my father when the rope struck me across my chest, jerking me backward; then, sliding across my chest, the rope hooked under my chin, lifting me over the pony's tail. Father made a grab for the pony's bridle, and missed. The terrified little animal went tearing away. I went with it, my foot caught in the stirrup. All I knew was sheer terror. I did not know that Father, rushing to the house, had seized his rifle. He believed that I could only be saved by stopping the pony with a shot. But both my mount and I lived on. After a frightening trip of about fifty yards, my foot slipped from the stirrup, and I lay dazed until Father rushed up and carried me to the house, placed me on a bed, and made a quick examination. No broken bones were found, only a mass of bruises on my behind where I fell from my pony, and sundry scratches and abrasions where sticks and stones had scraped and bumped.

"The cattle are bloating!" I finally managed to gasp.

Down in the field, Father "stuck" the bloated animals by thrusting the long blade of a knife into a stomach cavity through the hollow below the hip bone. Because of the bovine's digestive arrangement—cattle have four sections to their stomachs—the gases caused by contact of digestive juices with the new alfalfa cannot escape through channels available to most animals. Consequently, unless released by surgical means, the gases will cause such great pressure on heart and lungs that the animal will die.

Father saved his cattle and the wounds made soon healed. As for my injuries, after a few days I was back in the saddle, carefully avoiding clotheslines and keeping my shoe strings loose.

In his beekeeping enterprise, Father had done business with A. I. Root, an Ohio manufacturer of beekeeping supplies and publisher of the trade magazine, *Gleanings in Bee Culture.* On a visit to Arizona, he called on my father, and during a pleasant conversation I heard them discussing some items appearing in *Gleanings,* not regarding beekeeping, but of two young Ohio men Root knew by the name of Wright, who were trying to build a machine that would fly! They hadn't succeeded yet, but Root was sure they might, and had given them all the encouragement he could, even to an offer of financial help. I was quite excited about this. I heard Father say he was sure man's ingenuity would put him in the air.

"I hope I am alive twenty years from now. I think men will be flying by then."

Now I had something new to dream about. I had seen pictures of balloons flying high, and parachutes dropping from them. How marvelous it would be to be way up there, floating slowly down, and landing light as a feather. That's the way I thought of it, and hot desire flamed. I would become a parachutist. And if men got to flying in machines, that would be my life work.

The thought of parachuting filled my thoughts for a day or two. If I only had something like an umbrella . . .

My next thought was dark and devious. Mother had a nice big silk umbrella among the treasures in her trunk, a gift from Father on an Ohio Christmas. That would do it.

For a whole day I wrestled with the devil. I loved my parents. They were warm and loving even when worried by my misdeeds. I didn't want to hurt them, hardened though I was—but the devil won. At a time when no one was in the front room, I stole the umbrella and hid it under my bed clothes. That night, I sneaked out of the house and concealed it under the hay at the base of the tallest haystack.

Thought of my debut among the aviators of the world didn't keep me awake for long but I was up early, anxious for my adventure to begin. For once, Father didn't have to rout me out of my bed and I rushed about, doing my chores. I saw Father looking at me curiously. This wasn't like his number two son.

After breakfast I managed to slip away, unseen, I believed. I retrieved the umbrella and scaled the twenty-foot ladder, scrambling to the peak of the haystack's slanted top.

I had never been so high. I could look down on the roof of the house. I noticed the stove pipe chimney was bent a little sideways, the work of the last whirlwind. I could fix that myself later.

At the end of the topping, I could look almost straight down upon the spot picked for my landing. It seemed a long way down. How delightful it would be floating down.

I opened the umbrella and stepped to the very edge. As I paused for the take-off I heard my father shouting, then saw him running toward me, waving his arms.

"Herbert!" he called loudly and commandingly. "Come down!"

I couldn't have retreated if I wanted to. My feet were slipping on the slick dry hay.

"I'm coming, Papa!" I yelled as I jumped.

My flight was accomplished in approximately a second. The umbrella immediately turned inside out, and my landing, so far as my impressions went, was like that of a large rock. I was too dazed for thought for a few moments, and just lay there. When I could think again, I saw my father bending over me.

"Are you hurt, son?" he asked.

"My foot," I answered.

He was paler than usual, but after he found that a badly sprained ankle was the only damage to my anatomy except a severe shaking up, his face regained its normal color. The change didn't stop there. His face became darker, and as he helped me to my feet and rode me piggy-back to the house, mutterings came from his throat I couldn't interpret at the time. The translation came later and in words it was intended I should not forget.

It took six weeks for the torn ligament in my ankle to heal. The umbrella fared better. Practically undamaged, it went back in Mother's treasure trunk.

Everyone has had narrow escapes. In my case I have had a number of experiences which might have resulted in serious injury or death. But these were the normal accompaniments of life on the ranch or range.

The world's deserts are scattered with the bones of men who have perished in their waterless wastes. The causes behind these deaths include love and hate, search for adventure, lust for treasure, revenge, and fear. From among these motives may be found the impulses that drove Dave Miller into the desert beyond the Agua Fria.

On the morning of a scorching August day, a man afoot walked into our yard. Lyssie and Lawrence were out with the herd, Chappo was irrigating, and Father had gone to town. Mother, the girls, and I were at the house.

"May I rest awhile in your shade?" he asked.

Mother had me take him a chair. He showed and spoke his gratitude. The man was of medium height, with a gaunt, sunburned face. His hat was of the city type, with a brim too narrow to afford protection from the sun. His shoes were lightweight, the soles thin.

As he sat down, he shed a bedroll, very thin, a two-quart canteen, and half a gunny sack that had been suspended from a shoulder with a piece of rope.

At Mother's suggestion, I offered him a cool drink of water from the *olla*, which he drank eagerly.

"My name's Dave Miller," he said. "I'm on my way to White Tanks. A friend's got a mining claim over there, and he asked me to go partners with him if I'd come and help him out."

"But that's fifteen or twenty miles from here," Mother protested. "You couldn't walk that far in this awful heat."

"I'm tougher than I look. I walked almost all the way here from Phoenix yesterday."

My tenderhearted mother showed real concern.

"My husband is in town today," she said, "but if you'll wait until he gets home he might have a horse for you to ride."

"Thank you kindly, ma'am, but I've got no money for a horse."

"It could just be a loan."

Miller shook his head.

"If you'll sell me a loaf of bread and a quart of milk, I'll get along fine."

The bread was stowed in the gunny sack. He emptied his canteen.

"Ditch water," he explained, then he poured the milk in the canteen and completed its filling with water from the *olla*.

"The milk will sour," Mother protested.

"No matter. Clabber's good food." He insisted on paying her, and reluctantly, she accepted a quarter.

"Are you sure you know the way?" she asked.

"Sure. My partner told me. Go straight west till you near the hills,

78

where you'll find a road running north. It'll take you straight to the camp."

I got up nerve enough to speak.

"There's a shiny spot out there Papa thinks might be a miner's shack," I told him.

Miller nodded. "Bet you're right. I'll look for it."

Mother watched him walk slowly away, her expression one of deep concern. But with her means of persuasion exhausted, there was nothing further she could do. After Father's return that evening, she told him of Miller's sojourn.

"He is a fool," Father said bluntly. He shared Mother's worry, and he showed it throughout the evening. After evening prayers I heard him say, "I'm going to look for Miller tomorrow."

He was up at dawn. He loaded his spring wagon with several five-gallon cans of water, hay and grain, a bed roll, his rifle, and a box of food. The sun was rising as he drove away.

"I picked up the trail where he crossed the river." Father told us later of his search for Miller. "I followed it for a dozen miles, then I lost it. I used up a lot of time trying to find it again. I never did, but I found Miller."

In the afternoon, when the sun was low enough for its rays to reflect eastward, Father surmised that Miller had seen the reflection from the tin roof of the shack. He saw it plainly. He gave up the search for tracks, and drove directly toward the shining thing, which was, as had been surmised, the miner's shack. Flattened tin cans covered the roof.

Miller was in the shack, but he was dead. Father knew he should not try to take him to Phoenix. The interior of the shack was like a furnace, and his body was already swollen from the heat. The rest of the afternoon was spent in digging a grave and burying the man.

"I guess what Miller said about being tougher than he looked was true," Father commented. "But it would have taken a lot tougher man than he to have survived such a trip. He didn't have enough water and it was a hundred and eighteen degrees in the shade that day."

Father reported Miller's death to the sheriff on his next trip to town. Sheriff Allen knew Miller and Jim Gordon, the man who worked the claim.

"I'll let Gordon know about this," Allen said. "He must not have told Miller that he leaves the claim during the hottest months."

So the ugly, beautiful desert had found another victim. It was a long time before Mother could think of Miller's death without a twinge of conscience. Perhaps she hadn't done enough to dissuade Miller from taking his fatal trip, though Father assured her she had done all she could, as only force would have stopped him.

The instinct of the female animal to protect her young has made trouble for countless members of the human species. In one unforgettable incident, I came very close to being a victim of an enraged cow. With Lyssie, Father had cut from the herd a number of cows with calves and had driven them into a holding corral, where they branded and earmarked the calves.

At noon, Mother sent me to the corral to tell the men dinner was ready. The men, each with a pitchfork in his hands, were moving the calves into a smaller pen. I called, but in the turmoil caused by bawling cows and calves, I was not heard, so I crawled under the fence to get nearer.

Most of the cows showed no tendency toward belligerence, but one, with long sharp horns, was an exception. The men were safe with their pitchforks, but I was too anxious to deliver my message to sense danger.

The cow and my father saw me at about the same instant. Father shouted a warning and came running. So did the cow.

I whirled and sped for the fence, but I wouldn't have made it if Father hadn't met the cow head-on with the pitchfork. I made a wild dive under the fence, which had five strands of barbed wire, the lowest only about twelve inches from the ground. I scrambled under, the barbs ripping my shirt from collar to tail and leaving deep lacerations on my back.

I got up to see Father still wrestling with the angry cow, the tines of the pitchfork against her head, pushing Father backward while she bellowed her fury. The pain of the piercing tines finally caused the cow to give up the battle and run away.

Father hurried with me to the house, where Mother removed the bloody remains of my shirt. The wound was bathed in a weak solution of carbolic acid and a bandage placed over it, held in place by sticking plaster. There was no way to mend the shirt. Poor Mother. She had to make me a new one.

Ordinarily, one does not visualize raging waters on the desert, but they do occur following heavy winter rains or monsoon thunderstorms. The Agua Fria river, originating far to the north, would at times send down roaring torrents.

It was on a summer afternoon, following storms in the mountains. Lyssie, riding for strays, came galloping up to the corrals where Father was working on the fence. Lawrence and I were helping him.

"Flood coming down!" Lyssie called out. "It's a gully-washer, and carrying a lot of railroad ties!"

A railroad connecting Phoenix with the Santa Fe Railroad had been built from Ash Fork in 1892. This track came slanting down northwest to southeast, passing eight or ten miles to the north of our ranch. At times, when repair work was being done or a siding built, stacks of ties would be placed beside the tracks.

Father knew that a flood heavy enough to have poured over the rails and carried away the ties must be a real "gully-washer," as Lyssie described it.

"Saddle up, boys," Father commanded. "We'll all go down and see what we can rescue. We can find a lot of uses for ties on the ranch."

Ties were still coming down, along with a lot of driftwood, when we reached the river. Father laid down the place of rescue. He and Lyssie would ride into the stream with their lassoes looped and ready, and lasso the ties and drag them to the water's edge. They would drop those ropes, grab the ones Lawrence and I would have coiled and ready, and return for more recoveries. We boys would drag the ties away from the water. Then the ropes would be removed and coiled for action again.

This worked fine. The ties kept coming. We landed about fifty that day. Just when we thought we'd about seen the last of them, there came a lot more. The flood had risen enough to grab another stack.

We boys were working afoot, and Father had said to stay out of the water. But once I saw a tie that passed the men come near the stream's edge, I took a chance to make a rescue all by myself. In I waded to grab my prize. The water didn't appear to be too deep.

The sun had set, and dusk was beginning to creep in. Father and Lyssie were working hard, trying to beat the dark. At a moment when both men had their backs toward me, I made my move.

I had just reached the tie with water up to my knees, when I stepped off a shelf into deep, swift water. I went under, and came up spluttering, my mouth full of muddy water. But I hadn't loosened my hold on the tie. The channel suddenly became deeper and swifter, and my tie and I began a strange and frightening journey.

Lawrence, waiting for the next tie to be landed, had not seen me. Only when one stevedore instead of two was found at the wharf was I missed.

When I had recovered a bit from the surge of terror that gripped me, and cleared my mouth and vocal cords of muddy water, I began yelling, but my voice did not carry far over the roar of the flood waters. So I was embarked, alone, with no one to see or hear me, on a terrifying trip.

The channel became narrower and swifter. I could find no footing. My only chance of survival was to hang on to the tie, which was sometimes difficult because it was twisted and turned by driftwood.

If only I had learned to swim! Such an accomplishment had never seemed very important to me, as there was no deep water around. I had learned to swim maybe a dozen feet by a process known as "dog paddling" in the big stock tank. That wouldn't do me much good now, I feared. I'd have to hang on to that tie.

Suddenly, disaster. The tie jarred to a stop against an upthrust limb of an uprooted tree. As it swung broadside to the flow, the swift current caught the free end and tore the tie from my grasp. Quickly, it was gone.

I believed my only hope for life was to catch the tie. I paddled furiously downstream. In the faint light of late dusk, I thought I could see my beloved piece of timber only a few feet ahead.

My shirt and pants hampered me. I soon tired, and feared I wouldn't be able to make it.

I hit the tie so hard I bruised my shoulder. I grasped it to find it had been stopped by another tangle of driftwood. The end of a splintered limb gashed my arm, then the grasping current set the tie and me on our swift course again.

I felt the current slowing down. I found it was widening out. Soon my exploring feet struck bottom, and I began to work toward the bank. When I found firm footing, I looped an arm under one end of the timber and dragged it to dry land. Then, wet and shivering, I spread-eagled on the warm sand and rested. I tried rather futilely to drown out any thought of what the consequences might be of this latest escapade of the Youngs' bad boy.

I got to my feet after awhile, hating the thought of walking back in my bare feet. I found I wouldn't have to. I heard shouting even over the rush of the flood water. It came closer. I shouted back.

Father, Lyssie, and Lawrence rode up. Lawrence led my horse, and I scrambled into the saddle.

"I've got another tie here," I said. There was no answer. The other three horsemen rode off. I followed.

At home, I was last to unsaddle. The other three went to the house ahead of me. My clothes were about dry now. I heard my father's voice. He was talking to my mother and sisters, but as I came in, all conversation ceased. Mother had been waiting supper, and she and Fay now put the food on the table; all prepared to sit down. As I moved to the table, Father took my arm in one hand, my chair in the other, and seated me on it in the room's far corner. As Father seemed about to ask the blessing he paused, then said:

"Mama, would you please ask the blessing tonight?"

I had heard him make the same request, in the same tone, the day they had taken his steam pump away.

There was some conversation at the table, but not much. No one either spoke or looked at me.

When the table had been cleared, Mother filled a plate for me and Father motioned for me to come. I didn't have much appetite. Everything tasted muddy.

At devotions that night Father thanked God for having saved a loved one from peril. That punishment was the worst and probably the most effective I had ever received.

CHAPTER 10

Rawhide and Baling Wire

IN THIS TIME OF AFFLUENCE, THE DO-IT-YOURSELFER WOULD be very hard put to match the ingenuity of the pioneer in making do with a minimum of tools and materials.

Well housed, supplied with electric power and light, and in possession of a profusion of power tools, today's householder can hardly comprehend the scanty equipment with which a desert rancher faced his tasks.

When my father took possession of his homestead he had to add to the scanty, old, and battered lot of tools Wilkins left, but he never bought a tool he didn't need. With one hand saw, a hammer, and some nails, he built the addition to the one-room shack, the poultry house, and the combined tool house and harness room. With little else than a shovel and an axe, shaded shelters were built for the house, the horse lot, and the beehives. In that desert land of little rain and almost frostless winters, the livestock didn't suffer without waterproof covers. This more back-to-nature existence added to the hardiness of the domestic animals. I never heard of a sick horse on my father's ranch.

For the inevitable breakages and losses incidental to an industry's operation, the rancher had two invaluable aids: rawhide and baling wire. Rawhide was always available to the cattleman. For the rancher who had no baler, wire could always be obtained from the livery corrals.

Rawhide might be used for repairs while still green. One major repair I observed the men on the ranch to make was to a wagon tongue, split down the grain while the men attempted to extricate a bogged-down wagon from muddy ground. A ten-foot strip of hide was cut from a newly butchered animal. About two inches wide, this was wrapped tightly around the tongue in a spiral pattern. The skin soon dried under the Arizona sun, shrinking as it did so; as a result, the wagon tongue was stronger than before.

Hide had multiple uses. Door hinges were made of it. It was used as seats and backs of chairs. In emergencies, boots for horses were sometimes made of hide, Indian style. Rawhide lassoes—called *riatas* by the Mexicans, who were skilled in their making—were common. Chappo worked long and hard in making Father a *riata*, a beautiful piece of work that he prized so highly he would not use it. Instead, he coiled it and hung it on the wall for display.

For overall utility, however, baling wire took the prize. Among the uses that could be found for it were substitution for nails, bolts, nuts, and screws. Baling wire helped build and mend fences, as well as repair the handles of all bench and larger tools. On a wagon or other horse-drawn equipment, it was useful in wrapping loose tires, single- and doubletrees, neck yokes, and other parts. The tool box at the front of the wagon bed was improperly equipped without its wire nippers and hanks of wire. If a harness trace broke, a call would go out for baling wire. It could be used for hame-straps, or rivets in broken reins.

It was useful at the house, too. It could repair a chair leg or back. It could serve as wire to hang a picture. I once saw a loop of it used as a shoelace. When the wooden parts of Mother's butcher knife handle fell apart, Father took out his jackknife, cut grooves at each end of the wood, put them in place and fastened them with a loop of baling wire. It was then ready for another ten years of service.

As the use of baling wire was universal, so was its presence. It might be anywhere, as I can confirm by a personal experience. Once, while I was hauling a load of sand out of a river bed, a link of the trace chain broke.

No problem here. I would make a loop of baling wire, and go home. I went to the tool box to take out the hank of wire we always carried there. But it was gone. This was a crime, because that was one item that should never be left out. It was worse than traveling without a spare tire in a modern day.

Would I have to leave the wagon and ride a work horse home? It looked that way. But, more as a matter of habit than with hope, I would look around. I began circling the wagon.

I hadn't completed the first lap when I saw, protruding from the sand, a piece of baling wire. With a whoop of joy, I seized it and began to pull. Out came a long strand.

A listing of handy aids to the pioneers would not be complete without mention of the tin can, with special praise for the five-gallon size. This size was most often used to package kerosene for sale.

Kerosene, or coal oil, as everyone called it then, was the universal lighting fuel. But that was only one of its uses. It helped remove grease from skin, clothing, and machinery, light fires, and kill ants. Sometimes it was given internally to livestock and humans. It killed lice on animals and poultry—and so on and on.

In most places, there was no substitute for coal oil for lighting. Candles could be used in the cooler months, if they could be found. Father brought a mold with him to Arizona, and made a dozen candles with tallow. As soon as the summer sun bore down, they melted into a gooey mess. Therefore, as the most practical lighting fuel, coal oil was in constant use; this resulted in a never-ending supply of a useful by-product, the oil's five-gallon container.

There were so many uses for the five-gallon can that it is impossible to name them all. Cut out the top, make a bail from a can-wide length of a mesquite limb and some baling wire, and you had a receptacle better than a bucket for carrying water from the well. By cutting out one side, a wash boiler was ready for the fire. Cut off the lower third of the can, and there was a convenient vessel to put under the bed. A water or feed trough for the poultry could be made in a few minutes. Cut off the ends, split it down the side, and you have a sheet of metal useful for many purposes. Many a roof has been covered with tin from cans. Once, I saw a little homemade wagon, drawn by a child, with a side-opened five-gallon can as its bed. The isolated rancher had to be inventive, and the tin can helped him to be.

If a pioneer had rawhide, baling wire, and tin cans, he could take his axe and shovel and build a house.

CHAPTER 11

Little Cyclones, Big Breezes

ARIZONA'S WINDS IN MOTION USUALLY TRAVEL AT A COMparatively slow pace. We have been spared the smashing, killing hurricanes and tornadoes of many sea and land areas. Yet, once in a great while, we have had winds strong enough to be cautiously called tornadoes.

The mountains that almost surround the Salt River Valley help to alleviate strong winds. To the southwest, however, there is a gap where mountains are far away. It is from that direction that most of the winds come. The desert is a good breeding ground for certain types of winds, especially whirlwinds and sandstorms.

From our ranch to Yuma, there was almost a straight stretch of desert, with but few intervening mountains. We were in that area of scant rainfall known as the Sonoran Desert; most of it lies in Mexico, but also extends into that part of Arizona in which our homestead lay. It covers about a third of the state's total area.

Whirlwinds had a particular fascination for me, from the giant cyclone type that sent its whorls of dust and trash into the sky, to the cute little dust devils that I always liked to watch. On a hot day, I have seen one come skittering up to me, travel a half circle around, dance a jig, waltz away, then come twisting up to me again, ruffle my hair and cool my perspiring brow. Then, surrounded by a cloak of dried leaves and grass, it would dart away across the hot ground, seeming to grow taller and twirl faster as it fled.

It was the big daddy of these friendly, errant little vagrants that caused concern or even fear. Updrafts from hot sands of the desert can turn into spiraling, moving columns. These then turn into twisters that send roving columns of sand and debris a thousand feet into the air. Originating from the west or southwest, they zig-zag along the path of least resistance. Each summer, we could count on having a few sizeable whirlwinds cross our ranch, and we would hold our breath until they had gone their violent way.

Most of the time, these twisters had too much to do to strike us, but not always. I remember when a big one lifted all the covering from our shade, tore it apart and scattered it over acres of ground. While venting its vengeance, it took a swath of shakes from the house's roof. It then struck our haystack yard and twisted the peaked top from the tallest of the stacks.

The whirlwinds always fascinated me, though they could frighten me, too. I had vivid imaginings of being caught in a big twister, carried up and up in that raging black column, and then flung aside to fall to earth, a dazed and battered thing. As I grew older, that fearsome concept faded, and there began growing in me a burning desire to meet a whirlwind head-on.

I watched and waited. I thought I'd better not tackle one of the giants at first. Finally, the time came. The twister that was headed for a return to the desert north of our big stock tank was a tall one, but didn't seem too bulky. I cut out of our front gate on what I planned to be a collision course.

The plotting of my course was accurate. The little twister and I met with a roaring crash, or so it felt. My eardrums seemed to burst. The breath was sucked out of me and I struggled to keep my balance as my mouth filled with dirt and my eyes stung with sand.

The wind pushed me down, then pulled me up. My hat, a nice new twenty-five cent hickory number of which I was very proud, was torn from my head and went gyrating skyward. My shirt-front was torn open, then ballooned out and ripped from my back. My bare skin was battered with sand and sticks. A piece of broken branch struck my face and drew blood. I crouched on the ground and covered my face with my arms.

With a final *whoosh,* the whirlwind continued on its vicious way, as though having shown its superiority over the insignificant little blob of flesh and bone, it would now seek things more worthy of its power.

After some deliberation and seeing no other way out, I went sadly home to explain to Mother how and why the desert had yielded up her son in half-naked condition, leaves in his hair, sand in his ears, blood on his chest, and dirty all over.

Not long afterward Lawrence found my hat spiked to a saguaro, battered but still useful.

Though I have since encountered even larger whirlwinds, it was not with intent. My ambition had been satisfied.

Another type of wind that could have unpleasant, even fearsome, aspects was the sandstorm. One might descend on us in late afternoon of a summer day, always from a westerly direction. With the arid desert stretching far, there were no irrigated fields, no barriers to prevent a strong wind from picking up loose particles of soil and sand from the desiccated surface and carrying them along. There would always be visual warning: In the distance one would see a low, dun-colored cloud, which would rapidly grow darker and higher.

Sometimes the brunt of the storm passed to the north or the south of us, but if it came head-on, there would be a great scurrying about, fastening doors and windows as tightly as possible. The table would be covered with muslin; lacking cupboard room, it would usually have dishes, a sugar bowl, and other items on it. Muslin and canvas covers were used to protect the furniture.

We judged the strength of the wind by the height of the cloud of dust it carried. It might come with a roar, shaking the house and almost instantly bringing into the building the smell of dust, forced under the eaves and into every crack and cranny. A thick coating of it would lie everywhere.

By sundown, the wind would have died, leaving a haze in the air that might last for hours. If at supper time we found sand in our food and in our beds, well, that was just part of the life of desert dwellers.

Other winds came in season. Spring winds, mainly from the south-west, added to the aridity of the soil, shortening the season for those wonder beds of wild flowers. In the fall and winter months we occasionally had northers, winds that were a milder variety of the Texas "blue northers," those storms that "blew out of the blue to turn you blue," as a Texan once described them to me.

The monsoon season of July and August brought us thunderstorms with cooling rains. The moisture came in from the Pacific Ocean, the Gulf of California, or the Gulf of Mexico. Should all three ocean areas decide to favor us at the same time, we'd then be pretty sure to have a "gully-washer," such as the one that gave me that terrifying ride down the Agua Fria.

While an Arizona thunderstorm could frighten me, and a wind undress me, I think most often of those tender, dancing little dust devils whose soft fingers ran through my hair, whose lips caressed my cheek, and who whispered to me things I wished I could understand.

CHAPTER 12

Friends and Neighbors

IN THE CITY YOUR NEIGHBOR LIVES NEXT DOOR. OUT IN desert land, anyone living within ten miles was classed as a neighbor.

The voting district in which we lived covered about one township, or thirty-six square miles. A list of registered voters in this district at the time of which I write, taken from the great register of Maricopa County, shows that in our Orme voting district there were thirty-four registered voters, coming from fifteen states and three foreign countries. Only three of these gave Arizona as the place of their birth. Looking over the list of names I noticed two of special note: John B. Orme, for whom our district was named, and Charles Pendergast. We lived in what was then generally known as the West End, and our school was named the West End School, even though John Orme's name was officially used to designate the district.

Orme was already becoming prominent in irrigation and water conservation circles, and soon was to be nationally known. He was a leader in the move to interest the President and Congress to advance funds for the building of a storage dam on the Salt River. When the authorizing bill was passed, the first of many projects to come, it was signed by Theodore Roosevelt; as a result, the dam was named for

91

him. Had it not been for Roosevelt's prominence, it would have been named for Orme.

Charles Pendergast, elder statesman of the growing Pendergast clan, operated a ranch two miles up the canal from our ranch and ran a herd of cattle. He was one of our closest neighbors. When we children attended the West End School, there were more children with the Pendergast name than any other. Later, when the little one-room school house gave way to a more pretentious structure, it became the Pendergast School, a name that even now is prominently retained.

Snider, to the south, was geographically our nearest neighbor—unfortunately, not a friendly one. Between his house and ours lay a stretch of uncleared desert land. If he was married we never saw anything of his wife.

I was eight years old when my sister Fay and I became involved in a minor water war with Snider—minor because there were frequent disagreements over the distribution of water; some of these were violent. Since Father and Snider had come to an agreement about the division of the canal-end water, there were no further arguments, but Father had a suspicion that Snider might be cheating.

On a hot morning in late June, Father had started to town with a load of potatoes when he noticed the water had come down. The first twelve hours would come to us. There had been no summer rains, and the supply was low, so it had to be carefully used.

On this particular morning, Father told Lyssie to concentrate on the alfalfa fields. Lawrence and Chappo would ride herd on the cattle. Father had another job for Fay and me, an exciting one.

"I want you two to keep an eye on the headgates today," he said. "I don't want anyone else taking our water. Now don't get too near—watch from a distance. Mr. Snider will see me drive past his place and know I am away. If you see anyone fooling around the gates, run and tell Lyssie. Be careful."

Now here was an opportunity to display our talent! Spying on an enemy! Detecting crime! Preventing crime!

Fay and I waited until Father had time to pass Snider's place, then went up and hid behind some bushes, as close as we dared go to the gate.

Father's suspicions soon proved justified. We had waited not more than a quarter of an hour when, from a screen of bushes on the other side of the canal, we saw a figure approaching the gate from behind a clump of young mesquites.

"It's Snider," Fay whispered. "Look what he's doing!"

The man climbed the bank to his gate and raised it a couple of inches, enough to send a nice little stream down his ditch. Then he hurried away into the brush. I started running toward the gate.

"Papa said to tell Lyssie!" Fay called.

I scrambled over the plank bridge across the big box and closed Snider's gate by jumping up and down on it.

"We don't have time to tell Lyssie!" I panted as we sped toward the house. "He's away off down in the alfalfa and we were losing water." Our ponies were out to pasture, the day was hot—and anyhow we had the situation in hand, didn't we?

Mother seemed worried when we told her what had happened, but didn't see any point in telling Lyssie about the incident unless Snider came back again. We said we'd go on watching.

"Keep out of sight," she admonished.

"We sure will," I agreed.

I didn't add what I thought—that if Snider saw us he might kill us. I didn't tell Fay that.

"I'm scared," she said. "Maybe we'd better not go."

I was scared, too. We'd better have protection. Mother was at her washtub out under the shade and couldn't see me. The two younger girls were at play. I slipped into the back room and grabbed Father's shotgun and a couple of shells. When we got to our hiding place, I loaded the gun and propped it against the bushes, muzzle pointing at the sky. I cocked both triggers.

We waited and waited, and were getting restless after an hour's vigil.

"Guess he isn't coming," I said. "Let's go back." But just then Fay grabbed my arm.

"He's coming!" she hissed.

So he was. Snider came cautiously out of the bushes, looked around, then climbed the bank. Looking at the closed gate, he raised his hat while he rubbed his scalp. We could easily see his puzzlement, his wonder as to what he should do about it.

He finally made a decision. He must have thought the gate had dropped by itself, for he got a stick and broke off a short piece. He raised the gate and was leaning down to put the piece under it to hold it up when I felt a feverish urge to act. I put a finger on the top trigger of the gun and pressed it down hard—so hard that my finger slipped and hit the other trigger too.

The canal section in this photograph illustrates the type of water-control box and gate that caused the Youngs and their neighbor, Snider, so much concern. Note the crude road paralleling the length of the canal. Courtesy Arizona Department of Library, Archives and Public Records

That old gun sure made a noise. Two loud roars, in quick succession, burst on the air.

For a moment I was afraid, realizing that now we had nothing left to defend ourselves with. But I needn't have worried. The result of the double explosion was extremely satisfying.

From Snider's throat came a harsh squawking sound. He leaped to his feet, took a flying leap off the bank and, with giant strides, went crashing through the brush.

I ran to the ditch and again stomped down Snider's gate. Then I slung the gun over my shoulder and Fay and I ran for home, giggling as we went.

Father got home before it was time for Snider to take the water. Fay and I rushed to him to tell him of the day's events. When I told him about shooting the gun and its effect on Snider, he laughed in spite of himself. Then his face grew stern.

"So you forgot again my order never to touch a gun without my permission," he said. "Now I'll have to decide again how to punish you."

His voice broke a little, as he tried not to laugh.

"I'm going to the headgate," he told Mother.

"Can I go along?" I blurted.

He started to say no, then changed his mind.

"All right," he said. He told Lawrence to come, too. Though it was time for the change, Snider wasn't in sight. Father began to raise the gate when he came out of the bushes, shotgun in hand. He came up close to Father, the gun in the crook of his arm, pointing to the front.

"Now you see here, Young," he said in a loud, blustering voice. "I come up here this morning to see my ditch wasn't blocked by weeds, and somebody shot at me. Well, I ain't standin' for it! I shoot back."

The muzzle of the gun began to swing toward Father, who moved mighty fast. Like a flash, he was beside the gun barrel, which he seized with both hands; he tore the weapon from Snider's grasp and flung it into the canal. Snider looked away and half turned as if to run.

"Just stand where you are," Father commanded. His voice had more steel in it than I, for one, had ever heard before. "Now you listen, and listen well. First, don't ever, and I mean never, threaten me with a gun again. Second, warfare between neighbors is stupid, particularly in this case, where you have found it useless. No sooner had I left for town today than you came up here to steal some of my water . . ."

"Who says so?" Snider blurted.

"I have two reliable witnesses. They saw you raise your gate and let water through. After you left, they closed the gate. Later you were seen coming back, and opening the gate again when you were warned off. No one shot at you.

"Now, Mr. Snider, The best way for neighbors to get along together is to treat each other honestly. Suppose you try that. I will too."

I never knew of Father having any more trouble with Snider. I was happy that he and Mother both seemed to forget that time I had disobeyed. They didn't always forget.

Though Father and Mother eventually became acquainted with nearly all of the families in the West End, there developed only pleasant relationships with this group, no intimacies. Everyone seemed to be too busy developing their ranches and raising families. Most of the socializing was done at school and church affairs.

About eight miles northeast of us, on a small ranch near the village of Glendale, lived a family named Lockwood. They came to Arizona from a New England state. The widowed Mrs. Lockwood had five children: Alfred and Lois, then in their early twenties, and Lottie, Ralph, and Henry, all of school age. Of this group, Alfred Lockwood was to become honored throughout the state for many years as a justice of the Arizona Supreme Court, two terms as its chief.

Alfred began his career as a school teacher, studied law on the side, and was admitted to the bar. He practiced law in Douglas, a Phelps Dodge Corporation smelter town in the southeastern part of the state. He was later elected a judge of Cochise County's Superior Court, then moved on to the Supreme Court. Alfred Lockwood left a prominent mark on the judicial history of Arizona.

Mrs. Lockwood learned of the Young family, and, in neighborly spirit, had Alfred drive her down to the Auga Fria ranch one Sunday afternoon. Later, she visited with the five children. The two families hit it off well. Mother and Mrs. Lockwood became warm friends. Father and Alfred found their intellectual development had been along similar lines, and though there was quite a difference in their ages, they found stimulation in their disucssions. A close friendship developed, as was also the case between the younger element.

Our relationship proved to be a fortunate thing for all of us. While the busy lives of the pioneers allowed little time for visiting, we did manage to get together now and then. I remember that while Mother played the organ, Father and Alfred sang hymns and popular songs of the time. Father had a good bass voice and Alfred took the tenor part. Only one of these songs stuck in my mind, and it tickled me so much I never forgot it:

> Oh, the bulldog on the bank
> And the bullfrog in the pool,
> And the bulldog called the bullfrog
> A green old water fool.

Music of any kind was a delight to us. Once, one of the district's ranchers, calling on some business, noticed our organ.

"I have a music box," he said. "I'll bring it over next Sunday and we'll have a concert."

The instrument was played by turning a crank that revolved a cylinder from which projected a maze of pins set in a pattern. When the cylinder turned, the pins engaged projecting metal tongues that vibrated in beautiful tones as the pins depressed and then released them. With several cylinders, each with a different tune, this marvelous invention gave us a wonderful time. Mother then played the organ and we did a little singing.

It was during the general conversation afterward that I heard mention of two queens. Curious, I listened attentively. I hadn't heard of any queens here, but it seemed there were two. I heard the expressions "Queen of the Night" and "Queen of the Desert."

These two queens were the desert lily—I hadn't heard it called that before—that was the desert queen. The night queen was the night-blooming *cereus*, a member of the cactus family. Not only was it very rare, but it was very lovely and wildly fragrant. Now I had something else for which to go exploring. Through the days my determination to find the two queens, no matter what, grew to an obsession.

The things I had heard about the desert lily aroused the curiosity that later was to blaze high. One Sunday afternoon in spring I ran out of reading matter, and decided to look around a bit.

I saddled my pony and set out, riding first over Father's timber claim land. There were flowers there, but no desert lilies that I could find. At the site of the vanished steam plant I got through a wired-up gate, wired it up again, and rode out into the unclaimed desert to the northeast of our home.

I had entered a small grove of mesquites when I heard hoofbeats, and peering out from the branches I saw something I had hoped never to see. Indians! Two of them on horseback; one was a man, one a boy, both with hair hanging to their shoulders. The man had on worn pants and shirt, the boy was naked to the waist.

The same year Mother arrived, Geronimo was captured and sent to Florida. As a result her fear of Indians subsided, and Father felt free to tell her of his experience at Ed Kinnear's ranch. But after I became a voracious reader, I read some Indian stories detailing atrocities in lurid detail, and I carried a suspicion that the Indians we saw might just be waiting for revenge. Any Indians wandering away from their reservation should be strictly avoided.

That these two were on the warpath I could not doubt, as the boy had a bow in his hand and a quiver of arrows at his back, their points sticking up over his shoulder. My first glance revealed no weapon in the older Indian's hand, but he would have a knife and maybe a tomahawk, of course.

I was chilled to the bone, but not too chilled to whirl my pony, kick his flanks, slap him with my reins, and high-tail it out of there.

I heard a shout, and looking back, saw the two riders galloping after me. The man seemed to be waving an arm in a beckoning motion. Could he be inviting me to stop and get shot through by an arrow from the bow that the boy was waving at me?

It was a little better than a mile to the pole-and-wire gate at the head of our driveway. Looking back, I could see the two riders following me, but at a slower speed than my belabored pony was making.

Reaching the gate, I slid my mount to a stop and released the top loop of the pole and wire barrier, letting it fall. Then, riding recklessly over the fallen barbs, I went tearing up to the house. Jumping off the pony, I rushed into the back room.

"Papa!" I yelled, as I rushed to the guns and took down the rifle. At my frantic call, Father came in hurriedly. I had awakened him from his Sunday afternoon nap.

"What is it?" he demanded, taking the rifle from my hands.

"Indians! Two Indians . . . they chased me . . ."

I scrambled for the shotgun. In the battle that was to follow I would stand beside my father in the defense of our home.

I looked out. The two Indians approached, their horses at a walk. Father took the gun from me and replaced it on its pegs with the rifle. While I gazed in apprehension, he deliberately walked out to meet the riders.

Both Indians raised hands.

"How do, Young," the older one said. "We come to tell you . . ."

"Why were you chasing my son?" Father interrupted.

The boy spoke up. "We Pimas, friends. We didn't chase, we followed. My father wanted to tell him something."

I was astonished to find these supposed savages were speaking good English. My tension relaxed.

"We find dead cow with live little cow," the man said. He dismounted and squatted. "Brand like this."

With his finger he drew a Coptic L in the dirt.

"Yes, that's my brand," Father said. "We'll have you show us where the calf is, but first ask your boy to get down and we'll have a cold drink."

With glasses of cold lemonade in our hands, the atmosphere warmed.

"I'm Robert," the Pima boy said. He gave his last name but I couldn't pronounce it, so he said, "Call me Robert Smith—they do on the reservation."

While the two fathers talked, Robert told me of his life on the reservation. He had gone to government school, and could speak English and read about as well as I could. His father cultivated a piece of land. They missed two horses, and trailed them, but lost the trail and were on their way home when the buzzards led them to our dead cow.

Lawrence had a team hitched to the spring wagon when our visit was ended, and we all went up to rescue the calf. Father offered each of the Pimas a silver dollar, but it was refused.

"We friends," the man said.

"We surely are," Father agreed.

We shook hands all around, and the Indians rode away.

"I never saw that before," declared Father, referring to the refusal of money, "and I probably never will again."

Robert and I were to resume friendship in later years. His father was a leader in his tribe, and I had something to remember my wild ride by: the bow and arrows Robert gave me, with which he had hunted rabbits. My fear of Indians was gone.

CHAPTER 13

Quest for the Queens

SEARED BY THE SUMMER SUN, THE DESERT COULD BE A desolate place. Yet it was capable of magical transformation from bleakness to beauty.

Winter rains are not always copious, but occasionally they occur. When they do, desert stretches become a delight to the eye, with scintillating carpets of varied color stretching through the open spaces between perennial growth.

Father and Mother were students of Arizona flora, and we learned from them. On a Sunday afternoon, when the flowers were at their best, Father might exclaim:

"Come along, children, let's take an inspection tour." He would load the whole family into a wagon. On one trip he drove us down to the river, where there were wide stretches of sandy shore. There, we found great patches of white and yellow primroses, lavender abronias, and purple wild verbena. On the return trip, he drove through the half section of land which had been the timber claim before patent had been issued. The main attraction here was the golden poppy, the Arizona cousin to California's *escholtzia*. At that time, it was locally known as the California poppy, though California's flower is larger and deeper orange in color.

We all climbed down from the wagon and roamed. Still dominating my thoughts were the two queens, and I told Father I must find a desert lily.

"It's a little early," he said, "but we'll keep our eyes peeled. You can tell the plant by its long slender leaves with crinkled edges. The points of some curve to the ground, and when the wind blows it swings the leaves back and forth, leaving perfect arcs traced in the dirt."

Father and Mother pointed out and named other flowers. There was the Indian paintbrush, a parasite that chooses a well-rooted plant as its host. It produces a beautiful flower of red or deep lavender tones. Then there were daisies, purple lupines, and desert marigolds. I found a tiny, delicate white flower with an entrancing scent. Mother told me that it was a desert anemone.

The spring and early summer brought other desert blooms, medium-sized and with scanty foliage. When the desert bloomed, it appeared to be enveloped in a cloud of golden mist. The mesquite and catclaw put out fuzzy yellow blossoms that reminded one of hairy caterpillars. The mesquite bean, which provides food for man and beast, also provided a source of honey. Bees extracted from the mesquite and catclaw blooms some of the finest nectar known, and transformed it into a delicious honey.

The desert willow, found in the sandy ground near the river or in gulches, was an interesting tree. It had pretty little trumpet-shaped blossoms, each with a drop of nectar at its base. We youngsters liked to savor this sweet fluid.

The greasewood shrub produces a small yellow flower, and a stretch of greasewood field in bloom is a showy sight. The seed develops into a round fuzzy ball. The name "creosote bush" is derived from the character and odor of its sap. It appears to be of little benefit to man, though Father said the Indians made use of a product derived from it.

I noted on the branches of the greasewood little corrugated shells of some brownish or yellowish substance, about half an inch long and perhaps a quarter of an inch thick. These, Father said, were deposited by an insect of the *cochineal* family. Gathering these shells, the Indians made a dye from them, though not the bright red color made from the *cochineal* of the tropical countries.

Later, after having been informed by a farm hand that a good hair tonic had been made from the greasewood, I became interested in its possibilities. Perhaps I could develop a marketable product. Prudence dictated that I seek expert advice, so I wrote letters, and got one shocking reply from a university.

I was not the first one, I was informed, to have thought of the possibilities of the prolific greasewood. There had been many. One specific instance was cited: A man with dandruff concocted what he believed would be a hair tonic and a cure for his ailment. Without wasting time on tests, he gave his scalp a liberal dose. The supposition was that it removed the dandruff. It was no supposition that it removed most of his hair and poisoned his scalp.

Alas! My *Sunshine Hair Tonic*—which in dreams was not only a cure for dandruff but would stimulate the scalp and stop falling hair, restore its color, and make it grow faster, longer, thicker, and glossier— died a-borning.

Mother particularly liked to visit and roam among the desert flowers. Their loveliness helped her to overlook some of the inconveniences of our little desert home.

There was another species of desert growth that produced flowers of a type distinctly their own. These were of the cactus family. Our section of the valley was not thickly populated with the cacti, but we had a representative variety. King over all was the giant saguaro. We were not favored by many of these, as they preferred rocky hillsides, but we did have a few. They towered above all other desert growth, their branching arms raised toward the sky.

Next in size was the *bisnaga,* or barrel cactus, which has in fact and fiction saved many lives. I have read and listened to statements by men who said that the story of cactus saving lives is a myth. They ought to know, they would declare, because they have opened barrel cacti and found the meat dry, stringy, tough, and almost devoid of moisture. Such statements are made in ignorance of the nature of succulents.

In times of drought, cacti do use up most of their stored water, but they have an amazing capacity to absorb water when the rains come. I have seen the forest of saguaros north of Phoenix diminish visibly in size, then expand to larger size after good rains. The same is true of the *bisnaga* to an even greater extent; the lack of ribs such as support the lofty saguaro means that more room is left for the water storage that could well save lives.

The saguaro, palo verde, and jumping cholla cacti are evident in this typical southern Arizona desert scene. The Young family spent many happy hours exploring this type of terrain. Courtesy Arizona Department of Library, Archives and Public Records

There was the prickly pear in its many varieties, with round or oval pulpy leaves stacked one upon the other. Some trail on the ground, others rise high above. Among the smallest of desert cacti were the low-growing pincushion and fish hook, which hug the ground. Much different was the staghorn, with its slender branching stalks resembling the antlers for which it was named.

All cacti have thorns, some much more vicious than others. Fortunately in our area there were few of the terrible "jumping" cholla. This little plant is feared because, when segments of its long-spined branches fall to the ground and dry out, the needle-sharp spines become very springy. If a person should step on one of the segments near the tip ends it will spring up—hence the term "jumping"—and fasten itself in an ankle or leg with painful results.

All cacti have beautiful blooms, of varied bright tints. They resemble lilies to a degree, though with more and heavier petals. These petals are attached to a thick base that becomes the fruit. In most varieties, the cactus fruit is edible. Jellies may be made of it. The fruit of the saguaro was a favorite of the Indians.

In addition to useful and beautiful things that grow on desert soil is an invader, the tumbleweed.

Nature has devised many clever ways to insure the scattering of seeds from her myriad flora so that they may find new spots in which to germinate and grow. In my desert surroundings, I had opportunity to observe a number of these ways. Not only the desert thistle but also the mighty cottonwood provide their seeds with downy wings so that the breezes may scatter them far and wide. The seed pod of the devil's claw is provided with two curved prongs that eagerly attach themselves to the feet of beast or man, who unwittingly provide transportation away from the parent plant. Various plants have burrs that grasp at anything. Some plants grow along waterways such as irrigation canals, allowing the water to carry away and distribute the seeds. Cattle, horses, and deer eat the sweet pods of the mesquite. The seeds, some of which are not digested, are dropped with the manure. In season, this will help them germinate and give them a vigorous start. Birds also help the distribution of some seeds. But none of these have been provided with a better system of seed distribution than the tumbleweed.

Making use of nature's most prevalent force, this ubiquitous scamp of plain and hill, this prickly and universal nuisance has crossed continents, on its way climbing mountains, leaping canyons and rivers, invading farms and cities.

There are different varieties of tumbleweeds, but the common type is the Russian thistle. As soon as spring rains have moistened the soil and the sun has warmed it, the tiny seeds germinate. A plant forms, sending up a straight shoot that in its early stages may be eaten by livestock. Soon it sends out branches at soil level; as the weed advances in growth, these branches curve inward, forming a ball. These may be of large size, as much as three feet in diameter, but most of them are smaller. When the nights become chilly, the little prickly leaves turn color, and they are attractive enough to be used in floral arrangements.

When frost comes, the plants die quickly and the balls are then ready to break away from the roots, which they will easily do when the first winds strong enough to move them come along. Then they are off, rolling, leaping, tumbling, flying, scattering the multitude of seeds that lie along each branch.

Barriers such as barbed wire fences will stop some of them, but not all. A change of wind direction may set them rolling again, or an occasional whirlwind will pick them up and carry them away.

My obsession to find the two queens grew rather than diminished. In the spring of my ninth year I started the big hunt, spending all the time allowed me in its pursuit.

First I concentrated on the lily, for it would bloom in April or May, I had been told. So, on evenings and weekends when I was not assigned duties that interfered, I roamed the desert. A feeling of frustration began to develop.

Lyssie was minding the herd while Lawrence and I were in school, but we were often called to help on weekends. Occasionally I would be called to task for not keeping my eye on the section of the scattered herd assigned to me. Instead, I wandered all around with my eyes to the ground.

"But I'm looking for lilies," I explained, without effect. Couldn't they see the importance of what I was doing?

I had a feeling that Lyssie especially didn't care a chit whether I ever saw a desert lily or not, but it was he who bore glad tidings. It seemed to come as an afterthought on that Saturday morning in early May, just as he was leaving to saddle for the ride. I wasn't going to ride herd that day, as Mother said she had a number of chores for me. I was coming to the house with an armload of stove wood when Lyssie, on horseback and starting to leave, turned around.

"Say," he called to me, "I saw some lilies yesterday, across the river about two miles straight west. There are some mesquites close by, bigger than any others around."

I couldn't get to the house fast enough. I dumped the wood with a loud clatter.

"Lyssie told me where there are lilies across the river," I almost shouted. "I'll saddle up . . ."

"No," Mother said firmly, "I need you today. Now the butter is ready to churn."

"Let Fay do it."

"She's helping me wash."

"But . . ."

"No buts. When Papa gets home from town we'll talk about looking for the lilies."

It was a long day. After the churning I was told to clean up the yard. First came the tumbleweeds—a stiff spring wind had rolled them in the day before. These were last year's crop. Tumbleweeds had no season for moving. They would come from anywhere whenever the wind blew.

When the weeds had been stacked and burned, I had to sweep the yard of other trash the wind had delivered. I had done this before with a straw broom, but this took forever so I devised a new method.

I took a hatchet from the tool room, went up to the canal and cut a half dozen heavily leafed watermotie stalks, fastened these together with baling wire, and had a broom I could take wide swipes with. In short order, I had the hard-packed yard swept on three sides. Mother was pleased, and praised me for my ingenuity, which made me feel a little better.

Father got home before supper time. After the table was cleared, I asked Lyssie to tell him about the lilies, hoping what he told me wasn't a joke. He was greatly interested, and I found Mother really was, too.

"Why don't we all drive over there tomorrow?" Father suggested.

"Let's make it a picnic," Mother supplemented. "Fay and I will make up a nice lunch."

In the morning we hitched the team to the Studebaker wagon, packed in boxes of food and cans of water, and were on our way.

Not long after crossing the river, we sighted the mesquite grove that was to guide us to our goal, and after a half mile more of travel approached it. Lyssie had told Father just where to go, and suddenly before our eyes lay a sight that brought cries of delight.

Before us, in a saucer-shaped bowl the size of a large room, were perhaps two dozen gracefully fronded plants in full bloom; they were gorgeously beautiful. Even before the wagon was halted and we all alighted, a breeze brought to our nostrils the wonderful, enticing fragrance. This was a perfume worthy of a queen. Not then, nor since, would I wonder why this perfect example of the Master Creator's art had been named the queen of the desert.

Father and Lawrence unhitched the horses, letting me alone to revel in the beauty and fragrance of this wonderful bed of flowers.

On this day of discovery I could scarcely wait to finish the picnic lunch spread in the shade of a big mesquite. Then I returned to the lilies to indulge my euphoria, walking ever so carefully among those perfumed wonders.

It was, I thought then, the happiest day of my life. One of my goals had been reached, but only one. Could I find the other queen?

Father once told me that in our own desert country, at least, the lilies were inclined to be loners. While he had seen a few of them in past years, he had seldom found more than two together, and usually only one. Their bulbs were deep in the ground, and it was only in years when there had been enough rain to penetrate to the bulbs that they bloomed.

Now, with that patch of lilies before me, I asked why there could be so many together. He pointed out that they were in a little natural depression that held the water when it rained and retained the moisture for a much longer period than normal. Thus, the seeds of these beautiful lilies would have an opportunity to propagate such as would seldom be found on the desert.

With the end of May came the end of school. I didn't know whether to be glad or sorry. I hadn't made any real friends among the boys, and was too timid even to talk with the girls, who for the most part ignored me.

As harvesting time was coming around when school let out, Father took Lyssie off the range, along with Chappo, who had been helping him when needed.

"I'm going to make you two boys responsible for the herd for awhile," he told Lawrence and me. "You know what to do: don't let them scatter too wide; look for the best grass; don't let them mix with other herds; and keep strays away." There was enough fair grass to the north and west of us to keep the cattle in fairly good feed.

The country over which we ranged our cattle included that where we found the lilies. Little did we guess that on that ground the pretty town of Litchfield would grow not a great many years later.

I think there was only one thing that alleviated my dislike of the monotonous grind of tending cattle. That was the chance it gave me to continue my quest for what must be a very lonely queen.

Lawrence and I would take the herd out each morning and bring them back in the evening to water and pen them for the night in a large holding corral. Mother would make us lunches and we each had a canteen of water slung over our saddle horns. The days were getting hot and during midday, the cattle would seek shade under the trees. We, too, would find shade for eating lunch and resting the horses.

While riding, I tried to inspect every bush in the hope that a *cereus* might be there. The queen might bloom at any time during June and July, I had read, and could often be located by the flower's high fragrance. The trouble was, the *cereus* blooms only at night; the first sunlight withers the blooms and might destroy the odor, too. I developed a new daytime habit, sniffing the air as I rode. I found a new sense of the desert odors, and began to identify some I hadn't known existed. Maybe someday, and someday soon, I would find a new fragrance that might lead me to the elusive queen.

I'll have to do some night riding, I thought. That might be the solution. One evening after dark I slipped out to the mangers, saddled my horse, and set out for the east gate. I would ride northeast where the sage was thick. Lots of concealment there for the timid *cereus*.

At the gate stood my father.

"Has my son become a night rider?" he asked. "Do you have to conceal your acts from Mother and me?"

"I want to find a *cereus*," I said. "I think maybe you can smell them only at night . . ."

"Your ambition has gripped you so hard it is interfering with your work," he cut in. His voice grew stern. "It isn't safe for you to go riding alone in the dark, and I forbid you to do it. Unsaddle your horse and go to the house."

Frustrated and humiliated, I did as I was told.

After the evening service, I carried my cot out under the stars and soon was asleep. Nothing had been said about the incident at the gate, for which I was glad.

July came near, and we all looked forward to the Fourth. Father had brought some fireworks from town. Then one day something happened that for a time blotted from my thoughts the Independence Day celebration.

This must have been the second of July. Lawrence and I had driven the cattle northward onto the range that stretched to the Peoria railroad and beyond. Father had once ridden with Lawrence and me out there to a railroad siding called Beardsley, near an area now known as Sun City. It was a sheep-shearing camp, and we watched the skillful cutting away of wool turn a plump animal into a scrawny one.

The sun was low when we drove the herd home that second day of July. Lawrence would alternate between drag and right flank, while I did likewise on the left. Whenever I was out from the trailing dust I continued to sniff the air, trying to identify the varied desert odors and hoping for a new one. When we were about a mile from home, not far from the timber claim well, I suddenly drew rein. In the wake of a little dust devil that went dancing by, my nostrils caught a new and exciting scent. It was real perfume, and I felt great disappointment that it left with the tiny twister. I looked around for a landmark and noted nearby one of the few saguaros in the area. I noted it well in relation to our home station. I knew I would come back.

I tried to conceal my excitement during the evening, and guessed I had succeeded when nothing was said about it. After evening prayers I took my cot farther than usual, out toward the harness shed. I lay down without taking off any clothes.

After the lights were out at the house I waited awhile, then got up and crept to the tool shed and picked up one of the coal-oil lanterns kept there. I had no moon to light my way, but the brilliant stars gave me enough light to see by while I slipped up the driveway and through the gate into the desert.

I paused to make sure of my direction. Father had shown us how to find north by locating the big dipper. My saguaro landmark would be east of north. I lit my lantern and, setting a star course, trotted away through the brush and trees. Fifteen minutes later I had found my landmark.

I began to circle the big cactus, widening the distance with each revolution. It didn't seem to bring results. Was I going to fail again? But I kept on, circling wider and wider. Just as I began to think of giving up, a vagrant little breeze brought a whiff of that strange perfume that I had scented that afternoon.

A surge of wild joy set my heart racing. I began darting here and there, examining every bush. The scent would grow fainter, then stronger, then could not be detected at all, as the whims of the night breezes determined. I began to doubt my belief that I had found the queen. It might be something entirely different. I heard a rustling of leaves indicating a breeze stronger than those before it, and with it came that scent again, this time in almost dizzying force. The little gust came out of the west, and I hurried in that direction. Suddenly in the lantern light I saw a swarm of insects, attracted, I was sure, by the fragrance of . . . what? Different kinds of moths and other winged things had gathered about a large sage bush, and I rushed to it. Carefully, I began pressing aside the branches, and then gave a whoop of joy.

Exposed to the lantern light was a cluster of blooms in all its glory, flowers I knew could only be those of the elusive queen of the night. I danced a wild jig. Another dream had come true. The heady fragrance added to my excitement.

The flowers were lilylike, the white petals opening wide, a group of stamens rising from the center of each blossom like a little golden cloud. I stood there awhile, putting the full light of the lantern upon the royal cluster. The beauty, the elation, the strong but appealing perfume, made me giddy.

Reluctantly, I headed for home, hoping my absence had not been discovered. No stern parent greeted me as I reached my cot, and in spite of my excitement I went to sleep.

I was up early, giving, I hoped, the impression of an obedient, helpful son. I helped with the milking, then filled the wood box, ground coffee for the morning pot, and to my mother's surprise, asked if there was anything else I could do for her.

I felt some trepidation about revealing my night excursion and great discovery, but knew I just had to. So at the breakfast table, after Father had asked the blessing, I took the leap.

"I found it," I blurted out, my effort at casualness fading.

A chorus of "Found what?" followed as the whole family stared at me.

"The *cereus!*"

"Where did you find it?" Mother asked. She, too, had long wanted to view the lovely desert blooms. I told her. Father bent a stern look upon me, saying, "Herbert, I told you not to ride at night. I'm afraid . . ."

"But I didn't ride at night!" I cut in. "I walked."

"You must have known what I meant. I doubt if you found a *cereus*—it was probably a *datura.*"

"No." I knew what the jimson weed looked like—lovely, stinking, lilylike flower that also blooms at night. After I described what I had discovered, including the marvelous smell, Father decided to take a look. When Lawrence and I took the herd out that morning, he rode with us.

I found the place easily enough and showed him what I found. The flowers were already wilting under the morning sun, but they still gave off that strong fragrance. Convinced, Father noted other stems with clusters of buds soon to open.

"Some of these should bloom tonight," he observed. "We'll all come out in the morning to see them."

The next day was the Fourth of July. At dawn the whole family piled into the wagon and were in time to watch the Queen of the Night show a fresh cluster of lovely gems to the first sun's rays.

We stayed by the flowers, savoring the beauty and perfume until they began to wilt under the increasing heat. Father had arranged for two other hands to handle the cattle that day, so all members of the family could spend the entire day together.

It was a great day, and for me, a triumphant one. We had iced lemonade, ice cream and cake, and in the evening a big bonfire and fireworks, sky rockets, Roman candles, firecrackers, pinwheels, torpedoes. When we ran out of firecrackers, I got some of Father's gunpowder, rolled it up tight in paper with mud plugged in each end, punched a hole in the middle and stuck in a fuse that I had pulled out of a firecracker.

I called to the family to come and look at the result of my genius. Before Father could get there I had put a match to the fuse.

The bang I expected turned out to be a weak "pouf" as the thing blew up in my face. Surprisingly, it didn't hurt my eyes and skin very much.

CHAPTER 14

Feathers in the Desert

I FEEL SURE ONE COULD SEARCH LONG AND FAR WITHOUT finding another man who could claim that a bird saved his life. I can claim that, in all probability, a bird saved mine.

Despite the fact that the great southwestern desert has a reputation for containing vast expanses where sand, heat, and desolation predominate, these dry lands teem with life, not only of the drought-resisting plants, trees, and cactus, but with birds, reptiles, and insects.

No area in pioneer days was more prolific in desert life than the Salt River Valley of Arizona. The rapid encroachment of man has now destroyed or marred many of its pristine characteristics, but in the days of my youth, the area surrounding the Frank Young ranch remained almost in its primitive condition, the only change occurring from the occasional invasion of woodcutters and roaming livestock.

Of the many varieties of birds in the desert, best remembered are the quail, mourning dove, white-wing or Sonora dove, turkey buzzard, chicken hawk, night hawk, oriole, meadowlark, blackbird, shrike, woodpecker, flycatcher, ground owl, hummingbird, kildeer, and wild ducks and geese. Then there was the roadrunner, that friendly, prankish, sometimes insolent bird. It has a special place in my heart, as it has in the hearts of many.

All birds are possessed of talents of some kind, else they would long since have become extinct. The one I noted especially was the oriole, that lovely golden-breasted artist, weaver of beautiful abodes. The nests, woven entirely from hair from the manes and tails of horses and the tails of cattle, were truly works of art. The hair was gathered from barbed wire fences where it had become entangled in the barbs. High in a tree, suspended from a limb, the male and female orioles, working together, would weave a colorful basket; this was enclosed except for a hole in the side. The variegated colors—white, black, red, sorrel, and mixed—would be woven into a scrambled pattern that had real beauty. The orioles raised their families in these lovely homes.

Not all nests would be of pure hair. I have seen nests of other types of fiber, including string. The all-hair nest is rare, and it was the quest for such a prize that led me into another misadventure.

It was a bright fall evening when Fay and I, at Father's request as he was irrigating, went up to the canal's end to see that our headgate was free of obstructions.

A short distance above the headgate was a large cottonwood tree, with limbs overhanging the canal. In the late afternoon sun, I caught a glimpse of an oriole's nest, its soft glow indicating that here was a nest probably made all of hair. It was too late in the year for nesting, so there would be no young birds there.

"I want that nest," I told Fay. Under her protest, I began climbing, and soon was crawling out along the limb on which the nest hung. It began to sag.

"Herbert, come down!" Fay shrilled frantically. But I was close now. Just a few inches farther.

I didn't make it. The brittle limb snapped and it, the nest, and I went crashing down.

I had heard Mother talk of hard water, and now I learned that water really could be hard. The landing after a thirty-foot fall knocked the breath from me. I was in only three feet of water but I was entangled in the branches and dazed and didn't know how deep it was.

Fay got hold of the large end of the branch and pulled me to the bank. I scrambled out, soaked and muddy. The first thing I did was to find the nest. I was happy to find I had not been mistaken. The basket was woven solely of hair, and was as fine an example of pure art drawn from instinct as I ever hoped to possess.

Except for a bruise or two and a few scratches I was unhurt. Fay hustled me home for dry clothes and for whatever else Fate and Parental Power might have in store for me.

Among the carnivores of the bird family with which we were familiar was the shrike, sometimes mistaken for the meadowlark. Lizards and grasshoppers were its favorite foods so far as we could observe. Even though, on a good day, the shrike's storage capacity has been reached, that will not prevent him from looking to the future. An unwary lizard will be seized and impaled upon a barb on the top strand of a fence. Lacking that, the bird will pin its prey on a thorn.

The most prolific of our birds was the quail. As quail nest on the ground, where coyotes and skunks can easily make a meal of their eggs, it has been a mystery to me how they survive these ubiquitous predators and reproduce so profusely. A quail hen, laying at least a dozen eggs, will produce the cutest little chicks imaginable. They follow their mother in close file, and if an alarm call is given they seem to disappear, flattening themselves against the ground or in leaves or nearby growth.

An unforgettable bird is the mourning dove, or turtle dove as I knew it on the ranch and range. Its mournful notes had a strange effect on me. When out with the cattle and stretched out in the shade during the noon break, I always felt there was melancholy in the air; it could be multiplied by the saddening cooing of doves calling to each other from the mesquites. An almost indescribable feeling of depression would flow over me, and strange, perhaps atavistic, visions floated by. I was trapped in loneliness. Even now, the notes of the mourning dove can bring back those memories.

The pretty little Inca dove was much rarer than the mourning dove, but it did visit us occasionally. In those days we knew it as the Smyrna dove. The Sonora dove, or white-wing, appeared seasonally.

The carrion-eating turkey buzzard was the largest of our feathered desert inhabitants, also the ugliest and smelliest when on the ground. In flight, it was as graceful as any of the soaring birds known to the desert lands. Its sense of smell and sight are believed to be as keen as any of the earth's wild creatures, for nothing dead in the animal world escapes it, be it a mouse or a cow. From a thousand feet or more in the air, it can detect the delectable stink of rotting flesh, and aided by equally keen sight, it homes in on its repast.

The buzzard does not object to fresh meat either. I have often seen buzzards breakfasting off a rabbit on a roadway. The turkey buzzard has no fear of man. After all, this red-necked ugly bird, in his small way, makes the land and air a little cleaner.

There could scarcely be a greater contrast than between the buzzard and the hummingbird. Found even in the desert, these dainty little feathered friends most frequently had a black heads and iridescent green backs, merged with gray on their breasts and tails. The hummingbird used its long bill in probing for nectar in the trumpets of the desert willow and other desert flowers with protected pockets. How we children marvelled at the ability of this tiny thing to suspend itself in one spot while exploring the blossoms.

The purling cry of the nighthawk announced its arrival at dusk as it sought its supper of airborne insects. I never found out where these birds spent their days.

We had two varieties of woodpecker, the Gila and its cousin, the gilded flicker. The latter was to be found where saguaros grew. It builds its nest inside the trunk of the big cactus. Not finding room for its excavation between the ridges on which the thorns grow, the bird neatly cuts out a section of the thorns, then digs out enough pulp from the interior of the trunk to make a cozy room for a nest. This it lines with grasses. The saguaro helps its tenant by encasing the walls of the excavated space in a hard, durable substance, thus creating a permanent sanctuary.

Some say the little cactus wren, now by legislative act the official bird of the state of Arizona, takes over abandoned flicker nests for its own brooding. However, the natural home of the wren is inside the porcupinelike branches of the "jumping" cholla. It builds an elongated nest safe from any other living creature. As there were very few chollas in the vicinity of our ranch, I never became well acquainted with this little bird.

I liked the call of the kildeer, and enjoyed watching birds maneuver as they tried to lure me away from their nests, which would be built near water and preferably on ground with gravel and stones of a nature to camouflage the eggs. Such a place existed above our large stock pond, where the ground sloped away from the desert flat land down to the bottom ground. Four eggs would be deposited in a little hollow, all pointed downward and the points together. When I approached the kildeer's nest on foot, the hen would flutter away from the nest, beating her wings and uttering plaintive sounds as though badly hurt. I would oblige her by following. When she felt her nest to be safe, she would take to the wing with a defiant "kildeer! kildeer!" as though gloating over her skill in fooling that snoopy two-legged beast.

We had only two members of the owl family in our locality. The larger of these we called the monkey-faced owls, as the markings on their heads strongly reminded us of the faces of monkeys. They made their nests in peculiar places, most often living in caverns of some type. We sometimes found them in abandoned wells, like the one on Father's timber claim. They flew only at night.

The owl that especially caught my fancy was the little long-legged ground owl. In addition to being a nocturnal hunter, it kept vigil in the day time over its dwelling place, almost always a burrow excavated by a badger in its search for rodents. These might be found anywhere in the open desert where there were rodents for the badgers to prey upon; these holes were numerous enough to be a menace to the safety of our horses.

A pair of these owls occupied a burrow in the desert not far from our entrance gate. In my wanderings I had often seen the sentinel owl, the guardian of the manse, pop out of its doorway whenever its senses told it an intruder was near. This might be when I was still fifty feet or more away. He would hold his position until I was almost on him before retreating underground. We called these little creatures bob owls, because while watching intruders into their territory, they bobbed their heads, giving an odd kind of bow. In some sections these were called belly owls. They could be quite noisy in the evening.

One day, while circling a bob owl to see how close I could get, I made a surprising discovery. He could turn his head round and round without reversing it or changing the position of his body! I wondered why it didn't twist off. I was reminded of that one day while watching my father mend a harness. He asked me to bring him a swivel from a can under his work bench.

"What's a swivel?" I asked.

"Bring me the can and I'll show you."

He showed me how a swivel worked, its two parts turning independently of each other, thus preventing the twisting of a rein or trace to which it was attached.

"That's the way the bob owl's head is fixed on!" I exclaimed.

Father laughed. "It does appear to revolve," he said, "but it's an illusion."

Well, whatever an illusion might be, I couldn't believe it was. I went out to take another look. The owl popped out as usual. Standing, fixed on its long legs as though frozen there, nothing about its body moved except the head. I began to circle, my eyes never leaving those big ones of the bird. The head revolved as I moved. It moved round and round—at least ten times without a single sign of a reversal. His head just had to be on a swivel.

I reported back to Father, trying to convince him he was wrong. He wouldn't be convinced, and patiently tried to explain my illusion. After the owl's head had traveled halfway around, it reversed it with such lightning speed the human eye could not detect the movement. Reluctantly, I had to believe Father was right, but perhaps perversely, I called my little bob owl "Old Swivel-head."

Now to my friend the roadrunner. I have a special regard for this scamp of the desert and roadways. In great part, at least, this is because a roadrunner gave me the chance to save my life. After warning me of danger, he efficiently and spectacularly removed the danger in a manner few humans are privileged to see.

The roadrunner was so named because of its habit of pacing horse-drawn vehicles or horseback riders along the roadside. Also, unlike more timid creatures of the outdoors, it made unhesitating use of the road in traveling from here to there. If the traveler should make show of trying to outspeed the roadrunner, the bird would keep up as long as he could. If outsped, he would slant off the road into the weeds or brush as though he had planned that course of travel all along. But if he was permitted to win, he would pause, give a sort of bow, flick his long tail, and then go triumphantly about his business of satisfying his voracious appetite.

The bird is also called the chaparral cock, a name used without regard to sex. The markings of the cock and the hen are apparently identical, and I was never able to tell one from the other. The hen may be somewhat smaller, but one seldom sees a pair together. They are strictly loners in their pursuit of food.

The roadrunner has a rather drab dress of indiscriminate pattern. The feathers are dark brown laced with white, and the tail has a greenish tinge. His wings are stubby, their principal function being to increase the speed of his running should he be in a hurry. His eyes are encircled with rings of an orange color. When he pauses to look at you, he opens his mouth, the crest atop his head rises; the impression is left that the sight of you has brought upon him a condition of great astonishment or shock. Then, recovering quickly from his near collapse, he will go jauntily on his way.

Roadrunners build nests in large bushes or in the lower branches of a tree. This home is a thing to see. It is an untidy mess, thrown together with anything that comes to hand, mostly dead twigs and small branches. It looks like a pile of trash. But after it is tramped down and lined with grasses, it is sturdy enough, and will hold eggs. After all, one cannot expect all birds to be artists, can one?

The roadrunner is an explorer. On his forays for things to put into that bottomless pit inside him, he will range wide if food is not abundant. However, if he discovers a course where there are comfortably easy pickings, he may decide to take that way day after day. This was the plan of the roadrunner whose way led past our house each morning.

When the Brushwood Manor siblings discovered that the bird we named Roadie gave our home a daily scrutiny, we decided to reward him. I put a piece of board along his travel route about fifty feet from our front yard; the next morning I placed some cooked meat scraps upon it.

When Roadie came along at about eight o'clock, he paused to contemplate on this new thing near his path. After looking it over, he approached close and circled it a couple of times. Satisfied that it was inanimate, he tested one of the scraps on the board, tasted it, then quickly swallowed the lot. He paused and looked toward the house. We watchers waved at him. He made his little jerking bow and went on his way.

Lawrence shot a rabbit that night, and when he cleaned it he saved the insides. From these he chose the more edible parts and in the morning put them on Roadie's board. The bird circled at his usual time and wasted no time in cleaning up the board.

Each morning one of us would take out the scraps and come closer and closer to the board. Soon we would hold off until he got there and put down his food while he waited. One morning Roadie and I approached his table at about the same time. The bird, instead of waiting on the board as usual, suddenly started toward me in a peculiar crouching gait. I stopped. Was the bird about to attack me? I couldn't expect such an act from a friend, but what . . .

Roadie suddenly leaped toward me, and I jumped back. But so did Roadie, giving out a little squawk as a wing feather dropped to the ground. There was a hissing sound, the sound of scales on scales.

Between me and the roadrunner a large rattlesnake was coiling after his strike. Another step forward would have brought my feet down on the coiled serpent. The bird's intervention had undoubtedly saved me from being fanged—but why hadn't I heard the usual warning?

The answer to that would have to wait, as before my eyes was unfolding a tableau such as but few have been privileged to see.

After his retreat from the big snake's first strike, Roadie didn't wait for the enemy to re-coil its length, but sprung to an attack with a vigorousness that matched that of the diamondback. With its long, sharp beak, it went for the eyes. Quickly, the snake was in coil again and struck at the bird, who eluded the fangs by jumping backwards and to the side or back. Time and time again these maneuvers were repeated. Finally, with only bloody splotches where his eyes had been, the snake could not see his enemy. He continued to coil and strike wildly, however.

Now Roadie chose another target. Leaping in now with no fear of being struck, the bird went for the soft area at the rear of the serpent's brain case. He quickly dispatched the snake with a needle-sharp peck into the brain.

The family had gathered in time to see the coup de grace. When I told them that the snake didn't rattle, Father examined it and discovered that it had no rattles. Through some mishap it had been deprived of its ability to signal danger.

Roadie was waiting. I went forward and gave him his breakfast. When we gave him clearance, he advanced upon the dead snake and strutted around it twice. Then he paused, seemingly in contemplation. No, he decided, even his capacious craw couldn't hold that. With regret, I am sure, he bowed, flicked his tail, and went his way. With him went my eternal gratitude. Roadie, my friend, had saved my life.

CHAPTER 15

Creatures of the Earth

IF DEER OR ANTELOPE EVER GRAZED THE PLAINS OF THE
Salt River Valley they were gone by the time Father filed on his homestead. He did bag one deer, a loner off his natural range in the foothills
or mountains. No one could guess why it had wandered so far from
its habitat.

I never saw another wild animal larger than a coyote, that master
of the art of survival that can exist almost anywhere. He is wed to no
particular type of country. If he finds the land of his birth becoming
hostile, he will move. Even a severe climate is acceptable if it provides
a better hunting ground.

The local coyotes had no reason to leave the valley of their ancestors. There were thousands of them in the Salt River Valley. Jack-
rabbits and cottontails furnished the bulk of their food, though desert
rodents, even some birds and their eggs, were included in the variety
of foods they would eat. Like the human invaders, they loved chicken;
since our flock was allowed to roam in the daytime, we had occasional
losses. This desert dog joined the hawk, the bobcat, and the skunk as
predators of our poultry.

As a rule the coyote hunts alone, but now and then a strong leader will evolve who can gather together a pack, vicious and powerful enough to kill livestock. Such a pack once hovered around our herd of cattle, slaughtering calves. Poison was placed in a half-eaten carcass of a young heifer, and that pack was wiped out at one blow. The next day, seven dead coyotes were found at the scene. No more of our young animals were killed.

Bobcats were not numerous in our area, but now and then one would tire of the easily obtained rabbit meat and choose to breakfast on a nice fat hen.

The skunk, that odoriferous little animal with a stripe down its back, also liked chickens, though it seemed to get more pleasure out of killing than eating. He couldn't climb the wire-netting fence that surrounded the chicken yard, but could easily burrow under it. One morning we found three dead hens in the yard, apparently killed for the joy of it. He didn't get a chance to repeat, as a steel trap was concealed in the burrow and that and a shotgun ended his career.

Skunks are accused of transmitting the hydrophobia virus. But though they may be feared for that reason, perhaps as much fear is attached to their ability to pollute the air. Woe be it to the man, woman, or child who gets in his line of fire at a time of the creature's anger or anxiety. He can discharge a devastating volley. It is probable that only one thing on earth can enjoy the odor of a skunk—and that is another skunk.

The badger is an interesting animal, with his low-slung, solid body, his short, powerful legs, and his immense strength. His broad feet are supplied with heavy claws designed for digging. The badger subsists mainly on small desert rodents, but wouldn't pass up a nest of birds if he could reach it.

In going after an underground dweller, he goes at his job with all four feet, and can tunnel with such amazing speed that his prey hasn't a chance. I had proof of this one day when, upon seeing a badger enter a burrow that had been previously excavated, I tried to dig him out with a shovel. I trenched with as much speed as I could muster for a dozen feet or more, but I had no more chance than a rodent.

The open holes the badgers leave are frequent sights in the desert. In our neighborhood these were called coyote holes, as many of them had been enlarged by coyotes seeking rabbits or other prey in refuge there. The holes were a menace to livestock, both cattle and horses. A rider might find himself on the desert afoot after his mount had broken a leg by stepping in a badger hole.

One little rodent, the pocket gopher, was a great nuisance in irrigated areas. His mounds dotted the fields, where he fed on plant roots. Often, one would burrow through a ditch bank, making an opening for the escape of water. If not discovered in time, a section of the bank large enough to release the entire head of water might erode away. Consequently, trapping gophers was a regular occupation at the ranch.

Other desert rodents included the kangaroo rat and the wood or pack rat. The former was seldom seen as he feeds mainly at night; I have only occasionally glimpsed one in the daytime. He is well named, for he does in fact resemble his Australian cousin in appearance, with short front legs and long hind ones; he leaps along in the same manner. About the size of a small squirrel, he lives underground, excavating around the roots of trees and bushes.

The pack rat, approximately the same size as the domestic rat, builds its home above ground, assembling almost anything movable: twigs, chips—including cow chips—and dead branches. He has been known to pilfer household items such as combs, brushes, and tableware—but only when a home's occupants are absent. The pack rat's structures, looking only slightly tidier than a pile of trash, rise up to three feet in height, and are usually built within a bush, the branches acting as a framework. This little animal has been called the trade rat, as he sometimes, when carrying away an item, will leave another in its place. But it is improbable that in making the exchange he is motivated by any instinct of fair play. It is my belief that while packing some item for his house he sees another he prefers, and simply drops the one in his mouth and appropriates the other, not being able to carry both.

The desert air accommodated many flying things besides birds. Some were beautiful, some obnoxious, some liked the sun, some of the night. There were big moths and the little ones that hovered about our kerosene lamps. We had our beautiful butterflies and wasps that daubed mud or the more elite breed that made delicate homes of paper.

Of the stinging insects, the wild honey bee was prevalent when Father claimed his homestead, making homes wherever they could find an enclosed space, such as the hollow of a tree. Father early saw the possibilities in beekeeping, for the desert was filled with honey-laden blooms. Mesquite honey was recognized to be as fine as any the world produced. He started with a hive of milder-tempered Italian bees and gradually increased his apiary to forty stands. With extracting equipment, he filled and marketed his product in five-gallon cans.

I loved what the bees produced, if not the bees themselves. Honey with hot biscuits was a gustatory delight. When Father was ready to harvest a honey crop and he called for my help on the extractor, I insisted on a veil well-fastened down, and on having strings tied around my shirt cuffs, pants bottoms, and gloves. Even then, an angry bee sometimes got through my armor. Their stings were very painful to me and raised angry looking welts that were slow to go away. I'm sure the bees knew of my allergy, for I have been attacked at times when they were not angered by the robbing of their hives, and I was at least a hundred yards from the apiary. As I grew older, my fear lessened, but I retained my caution.

The family got some fun out of my reaction to the bees. Once, when at the well drawing water, I heard the unmistakable high-pitched buzz of an angry bee, I was sure he was looking for the best spot to wham me. The nearest cover of any kind was the row of figs on the near side of the driveway. With wildly swinging arms, I tore through the branches of the close-growing figs. Close by was a gap in the fig row caused by the death of one of the trees, and I crashed through it. Henceforth, with no record for accuracy, the other children would point out that open spot to visitors with pretense of admiration.

"We call that Herbert's Gap," they would say, and then to the accompaniment of giggles would tell of the race between the bee and me.

"The bee won," would be the final word.

The most common desert insect is the ant. While there are both black and red varieties, the large red ant is the most common. Their mounds may be found almost anywhere, even in very arid spots. They scour the ground far from their nests for seeds, edible leaves, or even other insects to lug back to their burrows. As I discovered many a time, they have a painful sting, the venom traveling to the glands of the groin or underarm. My worst experience with these ants occurred one hot summer night when I took my bed roll and moved well away from the house so that no possible breeze could be blocked. I leaped from my bed and did some wild slapping after a swarm of ants, crawling out of the nest over which I had placed my bed, began a vicious protest.

Another insect, many times larger than the ant but similar in shape, went by the name of "cow killer." This is actually a type of wingless wasp. Though one of these little creatures couldn't really kill a cow, their long curved stinger is capable of going deep and causing great pain. Though some have markings of black and red, the numerous short little bristles covering their bodies commonly approach white in color.

Were I to be the judge, I would divide the prize for genuine repulsiveness of all the crawling and creeping things of the desert equally between the scorpion and the tarantula.

The scorpion common to our area has a scaly body, claws like a crab, and a long jointed tail that curves up over the rest of the body. The big, curved stinger at its end is attached to a bulb containing poison. The sting is very painful, as both my mother and sister Virna found out, each having been stung on a finger. They usually remained concealed beneath shelters like logs, boards, or trash, but one occasionally invaded our house. It was wise, especially in cold weather, to shake out the bed clothes before retiring.

I never saw the yellow-tail or whip scorpion in our area, though it exists in desert land. Its sting may be deadly.

The tarantula, that huge, hairy spider so often featured in horror tales and movies as a symbol of terror, was plentiful in the desert, unpleasant to watch and frightening to the timid. They don't jump at you as some believe, but they can bite, although the bite is not considered dangerous. In fact, some people keep them as pets. They live underground, drilling vertical holes for an entryway and covering them with a trap door of webbing. They are seldom seen in daytime, except when driven from their homes, usually by heavy rains. In such circumstances I have seen many of them on the surface.

Another denizen of the desert, some of them poisonous but not particularly to be feared, is the centipede. There were in our area two kinds of these multipeds, one a huge, six-inch-long scaly insect, the other perhaps three inches long. Most of their legs have no other use than for support and locomotion, vertically or horizontally, but on back of the head are claw-like appendages, which when clinging tightly to one's skin will eject a mild poison. I know of no human in our desert country who has been seriously affected by a centipede.

The mild vinegarroon, which somewhat resembles a scorpion, is harmless.

The most frightening of all the desert creatures is the diamondback rattlesnake, and the ugliest must be the gila monster. The deadly rattler can be found everywhere, on desert plains or stony hills and rocky mountains. With his flat head, swollen jowls, and forked, darting tongue, he repels man, beast, and most birds.

The fangs of the rattlesnake are constructed like hypodermic needles: hollow, with openings near the end. The venom is ejected from sacs at the base of the fangs when a strike reaches its target. An example of the manner in which nature protects its creatures is the provision that should a rattler's fangs be broken off or removed, they will regenerate.

Despite the fact that they were as numerous on our ranch as elsewhere, no one was ever bitten. Some of our cattle were fanged, but they usually recovered. Our horses were more fortunate; they seemed to possess a deeply instilled protective instinct that warned them that a snake's rattling threatens great danger.

I know it was only good fortune that prevented me from becoming a victim of a rattlesnake. The snake's own warning system saved me on several occasions, but twice I had no warning. The lucky intervention of a roadrunner has already been recounted. I can only surmise the reason for my escape on this second occasion.

One day, when I was looking for quail eggs in a mesquite thicket, I saw a half-grown cottontail sitting before a bush. It did not move as I walked up to it. That was unusual behavior for the usually shy rabbit, and with aroused curiosity, I dropped to one knee to have a closer look. To steady myself I put out a hand, expecting to place it on the ground.

I did not feel ground. My hand went down on the coils of a diamondback.

I have heard of people being paralyzed by shock. I have never had that experience, and in this instance, with one wild leap, I put myself out of range.

Some believe that reptiles can hypnotize an intended victim, while others brand this as false. I think I'll join the believers, as I have always felt certain that the little rabbit's nervous system had been immobilized by the snake. He remained perfectly still until the rattler uncoiled and crawled away into the bushes. I did notice he had his rattles affixed. When he was gone, the little cottontail, acting as if in a daze, hopped slowly away. My presence seemed to have been unnoticed.

At times, seeking shade, the snakes would come close to our house. Twice, Mother came to the defense of her domain by seizing Father's shotgun and shooting the scaly invaders. One was about to crawl through the front door; the other seemed to have a similar target.

The desert produced another kind of rattlesnake, the sidewinder, which was in maturity much smaller than the diamondback. Its habitual domain was in sandy areas near water courses, though I have also found them in the open desert. That its origin was in sandy ground, where the surface was too loose to permit the usual sinuous movement of a snake, may be deduced from the singularity of its progression. It makes an irregular loop of its body, not a full coil; it then throws itself by suddenly opening the loop. The lower part of the body is then drawn into another loop, and the process is repeated. Thus, in loose sand or powdery silt, it finds leverage for its body's advance not granted by mere undulations. The sidewinder is venomous, though I never knew of anyone in our area being struck by one.

We encountered other snakes around the ranch, but they were harmless. The useful gopher or bull snake was there, though not abundant. The red racer lived up to its name: when disturbed it disappeared in a streak of color. There was a seldom-seen snake with black markings, with similar ability. The garter snake, common to most areas of the country, was another common variety. The little black horsehair snake, found swimming in our ditches, was truly born from a horse's tail, according to the solemn assertion of one of Father's hired men. For days, I watched some horse hairs I had placed in a can of water, but they never came alive. Gradually, as I grew older, I learned not to believe that all things told me were true.

It was a young gopher snake that gave me the thrill of believing I had made a great scientific discovery. No real snakes, Father had told me, ever had legs. So imagine my astonishment, followed by elation, when one day I found a snake with legs. Skirting the stock pond, in some weeds at the edge, I found it. No doubt about it, this snake had two legs sprouting out of the side of its head.

Father must know about this. I rushed to the house. Father was there, getting ready for the afternoon's work.

"Papa!" I shouted. "Come quick! I found a snake with legs!"

He laughed, but he came with me to the pond. The snake was still there, but its legs weren't as long as I thought they were.

"Kneel down here," Father told me after taking a look. "Get close and tell me what you see."

I got down and took a close look, which is what I should have done before. The snake had captured a toad. It was a little large for him but he was making a slow but positive effort to get it down. Taken head first, the toad's hind legs were sticking out on each side.

Of the lizard family, the most common was the little fellow one found at almost any place during lizard weather—in the house, on the house, on the ground, in trees, and about anywhere else. I have even seen them swim. They feed on insects, and will eat almost anything from a moth to a gnat. In turn, they are preyed upon by carnivores from shrikes to house cats. Roadrunners devour them.

The large chuckwalla is far less common than the little fellow, and sticks more to the lonely desert. Another member of this group is the horned lizard, more often but incorrectly called the horned toad. A favorite feeding ground is the ant hill, and it is usually in the vicinity of ants' nests that they are most often found. They are easily caught and quite tractable.

I had heard that a peculiar trait of the horned lizard was its ability to squirt a stream of blood from its eye. I had also read that this was a false tale. Well, let's settle that question right here. The horned lizard can and does squirt liquid from its eye, as I have twice been the target for such a discharge. I can't swear that the liquid was pure lizard's blood, but it was of reddish color. It seemed to cause no harmful reaction on my skin.

These lizards get their name from the rings of little horns which practically encircle the head. They have protective coloring, taking on the shade of the earth they inhabit. Browns and grays predominated around our desert home. In the red rock areas, I have seen horned lizards with coloring almost identical to their surrounding soil and rocks.

Though the gila monster is usually considered the most repulsive of all American lizards, some find a strange beauty in the orange and black coloration and pattern of its body. A formalization of the pattern has been used by the native Indians in rug and basket weaving and on their pottery. An adult gila monster will measure well over a foot long. With its ugly head, thick body, bulbous tail, and short reptilian legs, it can be a truly repellant object. This slow-moving reptile is considered only mildly dangerous. Its temperament is not belligerent, and it prefers to be let alone. It has small poison sacs at the base of teeth designed for crunching, so the principal danger to humans occurs if it has an opportunity to clamp its powerful jaws on a finger or toe. Venom might then be deposited by maceration before the jaws could be pried apart. However, as comparatively harmless as the gila monster may be, I considered it deadly in my youth.

The monster scavenges the area where it dwells for insects or other small living things. It also has a craving for eggs, a large one easily absorbing a dozen or more quail eggs with room to spare. Its mobility is restricted because it cannot climb. On two occasions, full-grown monsters invaded ground-level nests of our setting hens with ruinous results, crushing all of the dozen or more eggs in each of the nests. Once at night, I heard a hen making alarmed cluckings. I knelt beside the nest and placed a hand under the fowl, only to feel the broad scaly back of a big lizard. I leaped away, shaking. While I rushed for a lantern, the monster placidly finished off the eggs.

On another occasion, a hot summer day, I found a big monster just finishing a nest full of eggs. With a stick I forced it into a five-gallon oil can, wary of its jaws and not sure it might not leap at me. There was some delay in getting the can to the house, and as the sun shone hot upon it, the monster relieved himself of his omelet. He proved himself not to be a wasteful creature, for, after cooling off in the shade, he re-ingested his lunch.

Captured gila monsters were often taken to a curio store in Phoenix, where a dollar was paid for them. They were stuffed, mounted, and sold to tourists. Gila monsters were responsible for a memorable incident in my young life, the recollection of which sent chills down my spine for years afterward. Down river from our ranch was the site of a one-time stage stop, abandoned years before. This place was known as Coldwater, the English translation of *Aqua Fria.* On that late August day, Lawrence and I, searching for good graze, drove the herd down that way. In early afternoon, when the cattle were beginning to move out from their shady rests for more grazing, Lawrence told me to ride south and begin to turn them back toward home.

As I started to perform this task, I saw a rickety shack, all that was left of the old stage station. I decided to sneak time to explore and galloped to it.

Tying my horse to the limb of a mesquite, I ran to the shack. A door stood open and I went in, and found it contained nothing but a big nest of a pack rat on the dirt floor in one corner.

I saw in back of the shack remnants of boxing over an abandoned well. I looked in. It was gloomy down there, but I could see that the dry well bottomed at about twelve feet and that there was some movement there. I shaded my eyes until they became accustomed to the shadow. A shout of surprise escaped me.

At least a dozen gila monsters were stretched out or crawling slowly over the bottom. They were pale and thin of body and tail, but their color pattern identified them without question.

What a find! At a dollar each—my thoughts whirled. Why, I would be rich!

Could I get down?

The shaft was curbed with one by twelve boards, two by fours at the corners. The upper section seemed fairly sound, though the boards at the sides bulged in spots, and a few had been broken by pressure of the earth. The curbing at the bottom seemed to have rotted away.

There was a ladder built into the wall at one corner, the two-foot steps fastened at one end to a corner two by four, the other end to a two by four nailed to the curbing.

Yes, I could get down. And I would! I got on my horse and hurried back to the herd. That night, I didn't say anything about my discovery to Lawrence nor to my parents. After supper, I slipped out to the tool shed, sawed a four-foot lath in two, carved out a half circle at the end of each piece, and with a nail near the shaped ends, put the two sections together to form a crude pair of tongs. I rolled this contraption up in a gunny sack, and tied the roll behind the cantle of my saddle.

While saddling up next morning, Lawrence asked:

"What's the sack for?"

"To put gila monsters in, if I catch any," I told him. "You know we saw one last week."

Lawrence made no further comment, but I thought he looked a bit suspicious.

We worked the same area that day, as the graze was good. When the cattle began to move again in early afternoon, I moved south, and in twenty minutes reached the old station. I had everything planned. So that Lawrence couldn't locate me if he came snooping, I coaxed my horse inside the shack and closed the door. Then, with my sack and tongs, I rushed to the well. The rickety barrier around the top of the well impeded me, and I pulled at the boards, finding they gave way easily. I should have been warned.

I started down the ladder. My head was scarcely below the surface when a step gave way, and I plunged downward, taking out the rotten steps on the way. I went sprawling as I landed on the bottom.

Not stopping to analyze the possible consequences of this disaster, I looked for the gila monsters. Not one was in sight, and I could see why. All around the bottom of the shaft were cavities where sand had flowed out from a more solid overhang. There was room in those cavities for a hundred gila monsters.

I was very angry at myself for being so stupid. The least precaution I could have taken would have been to secure my lasso to something above and let it dangle into the well. Now how could I get out?

There were spaces between the cross sections of the ancient curbing. Maybe I could get my fingers and toes in these. The lowest section was three or four feet above the well's bottom, so I'd have to rise by my hands and arms alone until I could help myself with my toes. Stretching as high as I could, I got my fingers in a crack and got my feet off the ground as though I was chinning myself. Then I let go with one hand and grabbed for the next open space. I found it and got my other hand up. As I tried to draw myself up farther, the board broke, tumbling me to the ground. A deluge of loose earth followed and almost buried me. Choking, I scrambled out from under. Loose earth continued to pour down. I could see the cavity this left, taking away support from the ground above. What if the whole side caved in? I would be in an early grave.

I was so badly frightened now it was difficult to think. Dust filled the air. When it cleared a little I looked again. I saw the two by four to which the outer side of the ladder had been nailed. If I could pry that off . . .

I began to pull on the bottom of it. It came away—a two-foot piece of scrap. Then I could see that what I supposed was a solid section of wood was actually made up of pieces.

Maybe one of the corner segments could be used. I got the end of one across from the cave-in I had caused, and started to move another when a shower of loose earth came down, followed by a large chunk of the side wall.

Two scrawny gila monsters rushed out, coming straight for me. Were they going to attack? They veered off when I stamped my feet, but they stayed in sight. Soon others came out. Rats trying to desert a sinking ship. They continued to appear, one by one, until thirteen were present, of many different sizes. I yelled at them. They paid no attention. They would retreat a little when I moved toward them, stamping my feet, but they would come back.

They apparently expected the wall to cave in. If there had been only twelve instead of thirteen. Crazy thoughts began to race athwart my terror.

When I was being dragged by a horse no thoughts from the past had come to me. Now they did. I thought of my father and mother and brother and sisters, and how much trouble I had made, and how

I wished I could show them how I really loved them before it was too late.

If I was buried by crumbling walls, would I ever be found? And if I just died of starvation, and the gila monsters lived, what would they do to me? Would they . . .

My thoughts slid off that tangent. I wished I could see my family again. Would they cry because I was gone? There was a rushing sound as more loose earth came crumbling down. There was a crackling of splintering boards.

It wouldn't be long now.

"Herbert! Are you down there?"

I croaked something. It was Lawrence's voice.

He saw my predicament. He heard falling earth. I saw his head disappear from the opening.

It seemed an hour, but it could not have been more than a minute, when he was back and dropped a rope to me.

"Put that under your arms," he ordered. I wasted no time, nor did he. A moment later I felt the tug of the rope as Lawrence and his horse slowly pulled me to safety.

"How did you find me?" I asked my brother on the ride back.

"Tracked you. I saw you ride this way, and when you didn't come back I came looking. I had been sure you were up to something, and when I saw those tracks leading right into the house . . ." He shook his head. "Wait till Papa and Mama hear of this."

But this time, Lawrence was on my side. He didn't tell my parents about my brush with death until long afterwards.

CHAPTER 16

God in the Boondocks

IN ALL PIONEERING COMMUNITIES, AFTER SHELTER WAS provided, two other demands became insistent. One was a place where the children could learn the three R's, the other was a place to worship. The little country school house more likely than not would serve both purposes, and also as a general-purpose meeting facility: the voting place at election time; ranchers held their meetings there; young people held parties there. Once in a great while a traveling show would come and perform.

Church at the West End school house was the event of the week for many families. In their Sunday-go-to-meetin' clothes they would come from all directions. Denomination didn't matter. There were several represented at the school house congregations, and preachers from different Phoenix churches were invited to preach and conduct services.

As devout people, and endeavoring to raise their children with an equal devotion to God, my father and mother went to church with us as often as they could manage. If no hired hand was available for Sunday duty, Father would be tied down at the ranch and we could not go. Secretly, I felt relief, as I was always uneasy among so many strangers.

When we did go, preparations began the night before. The washtub bath was kept busy. Clothes came out of the trunks to be pressed. Even to this day, whenever by chance my nostrils catch the scent of orris root, or the faint perfume of dried rose petals, I think of Mother's trunk and the mysteries of its interior. It had a domed top, and in it her best clothes, and Father's, together with other items of intrinsic or sentimental value were stored, safe from the depredations of whirlwinds, sandstorms, and water from a leaky roof. How I longed to explore the depths of that treasure chest with its enticing odors!

Among Mother's treasures was a bundle of letters, tied with a ribbon. I got a glimpse of them once. The top letter, and presumably all of them, were addressed to her at Marion and postmarked Phoenix, messages from Father that had eased her loneliness during that long interval when they were separated. She was to keep them with her throughout the rest of her life.

It was amazing what that trunk had to give up. It had originally held several of her dresses, but their number gradually diminished. If one of her daughters needed a new dress or sunbonnet, there was material in a dress she no longer needed. But there were two familiar dresses she did not sacrifice, a black garment of fine material she wore to church, and a colorful print she donned on rare special occasions, as a trip to town or the arrival of visitors.

She had another dress, though, which she never wore but which she prized above all other things in the trunk, I think. She took it out to see if it was all right, and carefully rewrapped it in tissue paper. It was a beautiful thing with its delicate sheen and laces. It was, she told us, her wedding dress.

Once I saw her take out a box of paint tubes and brushes. She said to Father:

"I'll have to try painting again, if I can find some time."

"I'll see that you do," he answered firmly. "We'll include a studio in the new house."

Father kept his best clothes in that trunk, too, but another larger, flat-topped trunk held the children's garments. The everyday garments hung in a curtained-off space in one corner of the main room.

Mother had a problem keeping her family's best clothes neat and clean for Sunday school and church, day school in season, and for wear while at work. All of us were large for our ages, growing fast, and the source of problems. Fortunately, the line of succession worked pretty well for clothes that were wearable, progressing from the older down the line to the younger. Supplemented by Mother's needle, nothing was wasted. But new clothes still had to be bought.

One such occasion was memorable for us all. It started with the arrival of two men on horseback one morning, followed by Father saddling a horse and riding away with them. He returned about noon, seeming to be in an unusually cheerful mood. All he told us at dinner was that the men had come to inspect some cattle.

It was August of 1896, and hot. That night after supper, Mother went into the main room, lit a lamp, and sat down at her sewing machine, the little foot-treadle model that had done so much to keep the family dressed over the years. Father followed her in, saying, "No, Mama." He blew out the lamp, took her by the arm, and led her out under the stars, where he had placed two chairs.

"But you need the denims I'm mending . . ."

"We'll forget them. Save them for one of the men. Right now I have something to tell you."

Fay, who had just come out from washing dishes, asked rather timidly, "Can we listen too?"

"Certainly. This concerns all of us."

Sitting or lying on the ground, we all primed our ears.

"You know," Father began, "this has been an unusually good year for range feed. The filaree was high and rich, and the mesquite beans plentiful. The cattle are fat.

"Well, those two men who came out this morning were looking for steers fattened just that way—they make the finest-flavored beef you can get anywhere.

"I took the men out to the herd and showed them what we have. They were happy to find just what they wanted, and told me to drive them to the stockyards in Phoenix tomorrow."

His voice rose a little.

"And the price—well, they offered me thirty-five dollars a head.

"Well, my horse trading instinct crowded in just then. 'Gentlemen!' I said reproachfully. 'Do you mean to say you've come all this way to offer me a miserable little price like that? You can have them for fifty.'

"Of course, they'd have put me down for a sucker if I hadn't dickered. So we dickered. We finally settled for forty-five a head, twelve hundred and fifty dollars for the lot."

We're rich, I thought. Others expressed their joy in various ways.

"Now then, Mama," Father went on, "you may think I'm extravagant, but here's what we're going to do. I go to town day after tomorrow to settle for the steers and you and the children are going with me, and we're going to get new clothes for all of us.

"But that's not all. When we get dressed up, we'll go to Hartwell and get our pictures taken."

Two days later, while Father took care of his business, Mother, with all of us in tow, started in at the largest clothing store in town to make careful selection of the things her carefully prepared list showed were needed. Father joined in when he was finished.

With the seven of us carrying bundles, Father took us to a rooming house and engaged three rooms. We deposited our bundles and went to a clean Chinese restaurant for dinner. Then came the exciting time of getting into our new clothes and walking over to Hartwell's. It was after four o'clock, and clouds dimmed the sun.

We crowded the small waiting room. Hartwell was just finishing up with another customer. Then he looked us over.

"He'll think we're rich," I thought confidently, "with all these fine clothes."

"Who's first?" Hartwell asked. Seeing me fidgeting, a habit of which Mother hadn't yet broken me, though I was in my ninth year, he pointed to me. "You, young fellow," he commanded. I went into the little studio. Most of one side was glass. The photographer turned to Father.

"It's so late and cloudy I'll have to use flashes for the shooting. The powder will smoke up the room, but we'll open windows and doors." He went on to explain that the use of flash powder was a new technique, but a Godsend in low-light situations.

My squirming on the chair the man had placed me in stopped. If I looked pale, I probably was. Shooting? Powder? What had we got into, I wondered, and wondered some more when I looked at the contraption standing on three legs before me.

I saw a large, wooden box of polished wood, with a brass tube protruding from its front. A long black cloth was draped over its backside. Inside the front of the tube was a piece of glass, which looked like an eye staring at me. It reminded me of the malevolent glare of a bobcat Father had once cornered in the hen house.

"Do you sh-shoot people with that?" I quavered.

"That's right," Mr. Hartwell answered. "That's my portrait camera.

I have another for outdoor shooting."

"Does it hurt?"

"It won't if you quit squirming and sit still," Hartwell said severely. He adjusted a head rest and pressed my head against it. "Now hold still while I get ready to shoot you."

He stooped down and threw the cloth over his head. He stood still a moment, reached out a hand to the front of the tube, and turned it a bit. He came back to my chair, and twisted my head a little to the side. He went behind the camera, took from a rack what looked like a small metal frying pan, poured a little powder in it from a bottle. He took a match from a box. He picked up a rubber bulb on a tube and looked at me.

"Look ahead! Don't move!"

He pressed the bulb. There was a click. Quickly he raised the pan above his head, scratched the match and slid the flame over the edge and dropped it into the powder.

At the blinding flash and big puff of smoke which followed I let out a yelp and fled from the room and took refuge at Father's side. No comfort there! He just laughed at me!

I had to go back and have it done all over again, my chair turned half around. I bravely held my ground that time. Then all the rest had two exposures, so it was pretty late when we were through.

Father treated us to a supper at a restaurant, then we went to the rooming house, changed clothes, and Father brought the wagon around. He and Mother had talked of staying in town overnight, but decided against it. We wouldn't have the benefit of open air sleeping as at home, and the night would be hot. There was a moon and we enjoyed the night ride, arriving home by ten o'clock.

I felt quite grown up, staying up so late, a feeling that was dissipated before I went to sleep by the thought of what happened the first time I got "shot." I still couldn't understand how that box could make portraits like those I saw on display at Hartwell's. It just had to be some kind of magic.

When Father brought home the proofs of the photographs the following week, I was amazed and thrilled at the incredible likeness of each and every one of us. We were all extremely proud of the finished portraits, and after more than eighty years those of us who are left still treasure them as reminders of those days which, though fraught with hardships, were the happiest of our lives.

We had bought so many clothes on our trip to town that Father

The Young family, taken during a memorable trip to Phoenix in 1896. *Left to right*, back: Eva Young, 37, Vivian Florine, 4, Frank Young, 43; front: Herbert Vernon, 9, Virna May, 6, Elva Fay, 11, and Lawrence Leroy, 12.

had to buy another trunk to store them in. He was hard put to find a place for it, but finally managed to clear a space in one corner of the back room.

"Got to get busy on that new house," I heard him mutter.

I still remember Mother's expressions of relief that she was spared from the sewing and mending usually needed to get them ready for school.

Now I could go to church, I thought, and not have to wear a suit cut down from one of Lawrence's. I didn't much like going to church, but the Sunday following our eventful trip to town I didn't mind. I put on my new suit, but wished the time would come when I could wear long pants, like Lawrence. My pants came only to my knees, long stockings sheathing my shanks.

The other children all looked citified in their "store bought" things. Lawrence looked quite grown up, the girls pretty.

Father looked very distinguished in his swallow tail. His age, forty, and his years of hard work had not bowed his shoulders. He still stood tall, straight as a ramrod, and maintained the brisk stride of a man of purpose. His hair at the temples showed a touch of gray now.

Mother, too, had not let her dawn-to-dusk labors depress her spirit. Six years younger than her husband, she still looked attractive; her hair was dark and her features, unlined.

Our carriage was the then-new Studebaker farm wagon. Father and Mother sat on the spring seat up front, with three-year-old Vivian between them, pretending to help Father drive. The two older girls and the two boys sat on board seats at the rear, fitted over the wagon box. The wagon looked almost gay in its bright green, red, and yellow paint. The horses had been well curried and brushed, and looked fine in the new harness Father had just bought for them.

Father was in a happy mood. "Heigh ho, and away we go," he sang out. "The king and queen with their young princes and princesses are on their way to the temple."

"King and queen of what?" Fay asked.

"Why I thought you knew," Father laughed. "We live in the Kingdom of Spuds, so we are the King and Queen of Spuds, of course."

There seemed to be a special quality about the Sunday morning atmosphere, no matter what the season. There was a quiet that belonged to the seventh day alone. The last two miles of our trip to the school house took us through rows of cottonwoods, growing tall along ditch banks. Most of these had started their way to treehood as fence posts, and now had the barbed wire strands overgrown near the center of the big trunks. Once I asked Father, "How did they get the wire right in the middle of the tree?" He gave me a careful explanation.

The cottonwoods exuded a sap that had a pungent but not unpleasant odor. In season, a mixture of delicious scents came on the breeze from the alfalfa and grain fields.

In the spring, the trees shed their seeds, encased in little sprays of cotton. They were so light that the breezes bore them far and wide, in places covering the ground with a sheen of white, or piling them in airy drafts. The water in the ditches helped distribute the seeds, which would grow wherever there was wet soil. In the fall, their leaves turned to gold.

On this particular day, a friendly roadrunner kept pace with our leisurely one. He would pause now and then to see if we intended to race him. Finally he gave up and turned off into a field. Mocking birds sang on the trees. Now and then a flash of gold marked the emergence of an oriole from its green retreat into the sun.

The trip of three and a half miles was so pleasant it seemed shorter than it was. Many of the West End ranchers were already there or arriving with their families. Sunday school began at ten o'clock, and as we unloaded, the school bell summoned us to classes.

Tom List, superintendent of the Sunday school, arranged the assembly of more than fifty into four classes, separated as men, women, teenagers, and small children. List took the men, while the other classes had women teachers. Both school desks and benches from a storeroom were used.

I remember little of what went on in my class. I was in a state of confusion among so many people. I was scared I would be called upon to speak or answer questions. I had been, once before, but the teacher, finding me speechless, hadn't bothered again. I hoped, as Mother had said, that when I started to school next year I'd get over my timidity.

We had no regular minister for our little school house church. Perhaps once or twice a month a retired or practicing ordained minister might come out from Phoenix to hold services, or possibly a lay preacher. Now and then we would hear one of the arm-waving, shouting type who could stoke hell's fires until they roared.

When no preacher was present, a member of the congregation filled in. Sometimes I liked them a lot better than the preachers. They would tell stories and relate personal experiences of their pioneering days. I felt proud when Father took the podium. He looked tall and handsome in his swallowtail coat, stiff white collar, black bow tie, and well-brushed beard. There was an earnestness and eloquence in his voice that impressed me far more than shouting and arm waving. Such gestures as he made were impressive though controlled.

I can recall only one of these talks, and that only because I had heard the same views at home. Also, it was made memorable by his reference to a well-known agnostic, one who in my imagination resembled the devil himself, equipped with horns and cloven hoofs.

"That man," Father said, "claims that there is no proof of the existence of God. Such a declaration can have been made only through lack of study, lack of observance, lack of compassion, and lack of hope. How can any man of reason and ordinary intelligence not have seen a power beyond chance in the wonders of nature, in the delicate and gorgeous flowers, in the beautiful and fruitful trees, in the marvelous variety of animal and bird life? And most wonderfully, in the form, abilities, and powers of man himself?

"It would be a stupid man," Father declared, "who would declare that the wonderful mechanisms of the human body, with its myriad functions and organs working together and supplementing each other in perfect unison, could just have happened! Such a marvel of construction beginning with the miracle of birth could only have come into being through the design and will of that great and benevolent architect of the universe, God himself. In the marvels of nature, God can be seen everywhere. Look about you, Mr. Ingersoll! Use what brains you have, then deny if you can that God is everywhere."

One Sunday a frock-coated preacher from Phoenix arrived and spoke. What sufferings we all went through in those days. One must not appear in church without a coat, and if you didn't have a lightweight one, you wore what you had. This preacher must have had on winter attire. He sweated profusely. He waved his arms and shouted. He was really dramatic. I don't remember what he preached about, but I do remember I carried with me the impression of seeing a huge fire burning somewhere.

After the sermon and a hymn, we all went out as soon as possible, for it was stifling inside. The men and women gathered into separate groups. I stayed with my father.

I knew the names of quite a few of the men. Beside Tom List there was George Lutgerding, Hosea Greenhaw, Walter Kimber, Sidney Lowe, John Orme, Charles Pendergast, and George Wilky. Some of these names are still carried by their descendants in the Salt River Valley area.

I heard one of the men say, "That place he was talking about must have been in Arizona—Yuma maybe." The site of the territorial prison was already gaining a reputation as being next to the "hot place" for torridness.

The preacher finished shaking hands at the door and joined us. The men stopped talking about the cattle and hay markets, probably not wanting to run the risk of being told it was sinful to talk business on Sunday.

Jim Ivey cut off some comments on the weather.

"Parson," he said, "I heard a good story the other day, and being about a church I think you'll like it.

"Well, there was this little church which found that their hymn books were just about worn out, so they went shopping around to find where they could get the best price on some new ones. They was getting discouraged, 'cause they was poor and books cost a lot, when they got a letter from an outfit that said if the good church people didn't mind a little advertising they would furnish them a hundred books free.

"The church board was delighted. They ordered the books. They came. They were distributed in the church pews and to the choir, and when Sunday came everybody was smiling. The parson raised his arms.

" 'Brothers and sisters,' he said, 'How happy we are to have our new hymn books, donated to our church by a friendly publisher. The angels have smiled upon us, and to celebrate this event let us have as our opening hymn, *Hark, the Herald Angels Sing.*'

"Well, the organist played the opening chords. The parson gave the down beat. They all joined in, loud and clear, and found themselves singing:

> Hark, the herald angels sing,
> Beecham's pills are just the thing.
> Always sure and very mild,
> Two for man and one for child."

As Ivey's story ended all the men except the preacher laughed heartily. His face worked in a peculiar way and he put his handkerchief to his face. He turned away. He said in a voice that sounded half strangled:

"We should not speak lightly of sacred things."

As he moved away, he kept the handkerchief to his face, and I saw his shoulders heaving.

The men watched him go. The faces of some showed puzzlement.

"Now what in hell's so sacred about that?" one of them asked.

CHAPTER 17

The Three Rs,
with Dobies and Taws

IN MY FEW YEARS OF ATTENDANCE AT THE WEST END
School, I was beset by a good share of the human emotions. First there
was hate, for I hated school with an intensity born of timidity and
loneliness. I had one brief period of wild anger. I found a friend that
brought me hope and love, anguish and near despair.

Because of my parents' good tutoring, I did not start school until
my eighth year. Lawrence and Fay had enrolled several years before,
and were assigned to take me in and get me started.

With a dull heart, I saddled my horse that September morning and
went to school.

No architect had strained his imagination in the planning of the
West End schoolhouse. Hundreds of similar structures were built during the settling of America. It was the board-and-batten type of building, with three windows at each side, a storeroom at the back on one
side, and a utility room at the other. For winter heating there was a
pot-bellied cast-iron stove in the classroom's center. The classroom
could have accommodated perhaps fifty desks, but in my day there
was no need for that many.

On a small podium at the back was the teacher's desk, upon it a bell with a clapper and a wooden handle. It could make enough racket to call a noisy group of children quickly to attention.

A section of land was set aside for school purposes in each township. Our yard was a large one, stretching away into desert growth, but cleared around the building to furnish ample playgrounds. Near the back door was a well that boasted a pump. Drinking water was supplied by a pail on a bench in the utility room, a dipper hung on a wall above it.

For personal comfort purposes there were two outhouses, one for girls fifty yards to the southwest, one for boys a similar distance to the northwest.

We were not separated into eight separate grades, as in city schools, but by "readers." This was a system much like that used in the McGuffey era, though we used a different but similar group of books. We were given reading tests upon entering school. I was placed in the third reader, with competence in spelling, writing, and arithmetic assumed.

There was one woman teacher each year to handle all classes. Each year there was a different one. For the most part, these were to my mind stern-faced and grim, ever ready with a sharp tongue, and on occasion a paddle. There was no thought then of legislation to curb this method of disciplining errant youth. Rather, a parent would likely accept the teacher's judgment as correct and punish the wayward offspring again when he got home.

Familiarity performed its traditional function, and by the end of the first term I was shedding my timidity and getting along fairly well in classes. During noon hours and recess periods, I began to join the younger group in some of their activities. The older boys usually had a baseball game going, and Lawrence was involved in this, so he paid no attention to what I was doing; I was glad of this when I became involved in a sinful sport. Doubly sinful, because I was not only to be involved in a gambling game, always a wicked thing, but because I was disobeying my mother's wishes.

I was fascinated by the game of marbles. In my first year at school I merely watched, learning the game's intricacies. I asked my father to get me some marbles, and he brought me a bag of twenty-five "dobies," with a glass "taw." Seeing the transaction, Mother warned me against playing for "keeps" as that would be gambling.

I began practicing shooting marbles. I kept at it during the summer vacation whenever I had time to spare. When school came, I felt I was good enough to join the other marble players, who lost no time in getting at it that Monday noon. They ignored me, and I was afraid to ask. So I found a bare spot out of the way and began to practice by myself. It was then I met Max, who developed into the first real enemy I had ever had. Max was a boy perhaps a year older than I, but broader and heavier. He was in my classes at school, and formed a dislike for me after I had twiced spelled him down in the spelling matches. These were the kind where pupils are lined up and went to the foot if they missed a word. Max didn't like to be beaten at anything. He showed his dislike by a sneer at every excuse, even making fun of my clothes.

Max was one of the best shots at school at marbles. If he thought he could gain by it, he wasn't averse to cheating by failing to keep "knucks down" or "fudging." If any of the boys protested, he would threaten them.

Though each school developed its own rules, at West End an oval ring was first drawn in the dirt and each player put in an agreed-upon number of marbles. Then they would "lag"—toss marbles, usually their shooting taw—toward a line some distance away, the closest winning first toss at the ring for shooting position. The others would toss toward the ring in turn, being careful to keep their taws outside the ring. They would maintain the same shooting order throughout the game. Play began by shooting at the dobies in the ring or at an opponent's taw outside the ring. Each player kept the marbles he knocked out of the ring. If another player's taw was close, that player could be "killed," or put out of the game by hitting it with his own taw. If the taw remained in the ring after a shot, it was "dead"— putting the owner out of the game, with a loss of all his remaining marbles.

To see that I possessed marbles was all Max needed to arouse his cupidity. It was easy enought to interpret his thought processes. Here was a sucker ready for the kill. As the morning recess game ended, he stalked over to me. "Get in the game at noon." His words carried command.

For that tone, I almost stayed out, but temptation was too great. After hastily eaten lunches, the marble shooters assembled for battle, and I was there with the ten marbles I brought from home and the clumsy glass taw so different from the beautiful agate taws most of the boys had.

I was nervous in that first game of "keeps," which I realized took from me my boyhood innocence and made of me a gambler.

144

For the rest of the day a fog of guilt hung around me, intensified by the ignominy of having lost all my marbles in the first ten minutes of play. I fumbled my shots. Through it all I could see the sneering face of Max and hear his jeers at my ineptness. In my gloom I came to a decision to end my marble playing career then and there.

The next morning I put all the rest of my marbles in my pocket, and at noon joined the game. It took longer this time. I held out for thirty minutes. I had my taw left, but it was useless now.

The next day at noon a boy named Willie, one of those responsible for my destitute condition, greedily eyed the apple Mother had included with my sandwich and cake.

"Give you five marbles for the apple," he said.

I succumbed. I joined the other gamblers and after winning one game, I lost the next two. Max sneered at my inability to win.

If I was a little heavier, I thought, mentally using some of the slang I was picking up at school, I'd have popped him in the kisser.

I began blaming my losses on my taw, a piece of glass with whorls in it that twisted to look like a glaring, evil-looking eye. When Willie offered me a marbles-for-apple trade next day I said, "Not enough."

"What do you want?"

"Your aggie taw."

He wailed like I had asked for his life's blood. There was no trade. Next day Willie brought an agate to school and showed it to me. It was just what I wanted except on one side it had been chipped, leaving a small flat place.

I tried it. The flat place when put under the tip of my index finger felt just right, but I didn't tell Willie that. I gave it back, telling him I hadn't been looking for a broken taw.

"Give it for your apple," he offered.

We dickered. He must have been hungry, for I finally got the taw and five marbles for my apple. I hurried off to join the game.

All my hours of practice paid off in the magic of my aggie. It seemed like I couldn't miss. When the bell rang I had a pocket loaded with marbles.

After that, I won more than I lost. I came to love my aggie, which performed better and better at greater and greater distances. There was seldom a day that I could not add to my secret hoard. For awhile my success surrounded me with a sort of euphoria, but this ended and my conscience began to nag me when Willie dropped out, saying he had no more marbles. Then another quit, than another. Harry and Johnny, two of the older boys, and Max and I were left as the only players. Something was very wrong here. Three boys had been forced to become onlookers at a game they loved.

Max's meanness bothered me, too. He continued to accuse me of failing to keep knucks down or fudging whenever I made a successful shot. Finally, Harry and Johnny began to emulate his tactics whenever he made a good shot. This enraged him, but he finally got the message.

The fall term was nearing a close when Johnny made a suggestion the other players eagerly grasped. Max had just won a game in which he and I had been finalists.

"Let's get up a championship game between Max and Herb," Johnny said.

"With a big ring, fifty marbles apiece in it," Harry supplemented.

There was no way for me to back out. I didn't want to play a game with maybe everyone in the school looking on. Lawrence and Fay would know. Lawrence had been too occupied with baseball ever to watch a marble game, and he now would learn that I was gambling. I suddenly began to hate the game that had got me into this. My feeling of guilt continued to expand. This would hurt my parents terribly.

Max, who had quickly agreed to the match, began to brag about what he would do to me. My inner rage told me that there must be a reckoning some day.

Harry, Johnny, and other players quickly set up the game plan. Each contestant would place fifty marbles in an oval ring that was three feet long and half that wide in the middle, and tapered to a point at the ends. The lag line would be extended. First lag by lot. First one to fudge or show knucks-up would be declared loser.

Harry and Johnny would be judges.

Riding home that evening, Lawrence said:

"It's being talked around you and Max are going to play marbles to see who's champion, and each is to put up fifty marbles. Does that mean you'll be playing for keeps?"

"Yes."

"Do Papa and Mama know?"

"I never told them."

"Are you going to? Because if you don't I think I'll have to."

"I'm going to tell them myself tomorrow night. I've got to play that game. Please don't say anything before that."

Before I went to sleep that night, I had made up my mind what I had to do. The next morning early I got a gunny sack, hastily dug up my entire hoard of marbles and dumped them into it. When I saddled up I tied the sack behind the cantle.

That morning at school I was reprimanded by Mrs. Wilson, my teacher, for not paying attention. My mind was filled with trepidation over the pending contest and the inevitable aftermath.

At twelve o'clock, all the boys of the marble team swallowed their lunches in a hurry and rushed to the marble court. I brought my sack. Harry and Johnny quickly laid out the ring and a lag line fifty feet from it. Max and I put in our marbles. Play was commenced.

A crowd consisting of most of the students in the school gathered. My nervousness grew. I wasn't mentally equipped for this sort of thing. Max was, or at least pretended to be, overflowing with confidence.

We drew straws for the first lag. I won and made a bad job of it. Max easily won first throw to the ring.

The strategy called for was to aim just off the end of the ring; if the taw went too far it wouldn't go fat, that is, enter the ring and become dead, putting the player out of the game. Max tried for the left end, and his taw went three feet past it. I tried for the other end and wound up two feet short. Max carefully shot back to the edge of the ring, in fine position to begin skinning, or knocking marbles out of the ring.

My taw was too far back for me to try skinning with certainty, and if I played just for position Max might skin across and kill my taw.

What could I do to stay alive and still play safe? To kill a little time I got down and squinted across the ring at Max's taw. It was a beautiful aggie, a little larger than mine, and beautifully marked. The overhead sun was reflected from it in a way that made it appear like a glaring eye. It reminded me of Max's hateful eyes when he glared at me.

I suddenly made up my mind. I couldn't stand the strain of the match accentuated by the talkative, watching crowd. I'd have to get this over with. Losing wasn't the worst thing in the world since it would get me away from there.

I would go for Max's taw!

I carefully positioned myself. The judges watched closely. I grasped my taw between thumb and forefinger and then looked across the ring. The enemy taw was five feet away.

I had never tried a five-foot shot while in play. I had made some, missed some, at three feet. Suddenly that shining target seemed in just the right place. I let go.

Crack! My taw hit Max's squarely, taking its place while it skittered a foot away.

A shout went up which made me even more nervous. It appeared the boys and girls had favored me! I couldn't believe it. Max apparently refused to believe what had happened. He kept muttering something about fudging and knucks-up until Harry and Johnny grabbed his arms.

"You rotten sport!" I heard Harry hiss. "That was a good, clean shot, and you know it! Now shut up!"

Johnny said, "We'll help you pick up your marbles." I got my sack. Max stood glowering at me.

"Take your marbles back," I said, "I don't want them."

Max took a step forward, than at Harry's "No!" suddenly stopped.

"I don't want 'em," he said. "I've got lots of marbles."

I handed the sack to Johnny.

"I'm not going to play any more," I said. "Please divide these evenly among you five players." I indicated all but Max.

"What about me?" Max complained.

"You have lots of marbles," I said.

The other boys protested, but I convinced them I would not play again. I gave the championship taw back to Willie.

I got so many congratulations it made me feel silly. As the crowd melted away, I heard one boy say:

"Gosh, what a shot! At least six feet away!"

"More like seven," another boy said. "Maybe more."

Thus at age nine, goin' on ten, I became the boy who won the West End marble championship by, it was said, a killing shot of ten feet.

There should have been great satisfaction in beating the big bully Max, but that was overshadowed by worry over what was to come.

All the way through supper that evening I tried to think of a way to start my confession when Mother solved that problem. She asked, "I saw you riding away with a sack tied behind your saddle. What was in it?"

"Marbles." It would come easier now.

"But Papa got you only a few."

"I had over three hundred. I won them playing keeps."

Mother looked shocked. She stared at me a little while, then tears filled her eyes.

"But Herbert, I told you . . ."

Father looked stern, but he knew there was more to explain before my trial was over.

"What did you do with the marbles?" he demanded.

"I gave them all back to the boys I won them from."

Father arose, came around the table and placed his arm across my shoulders. He hugged me, and Mother did too.

"Mama," Father said, "I think our boy is growing up."

"It wasn't the teacher, it was the system." Going to school meant, in theory at least, six hours of study from books crammed with facts and problems. The teacher could have brightened things up by an occasional little story or anecdote pertinent to the study being pursued, but they didn't train teachers that way. Not Miss Wilson, anyway, nor any of the other teachers I had.

So I found school very dull, and learned to dislike it. There was no part of the curriculum to entice a dreamer. I got through the first half of the year after a fashion and the Christmas vacation period I longed for finally approached. At the end of each term, there were recitations or other exercises by the students, and all the parents were invited.

In making up her program, Miss Wilson told me I was to "speak a piece," and gave me a poem with a Christmas theme. There would be songs, both solo and in chorus, recitations, and a play for the older pupils, in which both Lawrence and Fay had a part.

I had no trouble learning my piece, and as I had recited other pieces at other programs, I thought maybe I could get through this one without muffing it. But I didn't. All because of a girl with blue eyes and yellow hair.

For such events all the pupils were to be seated as in school. Several rows of benches were placed behind the school desks for parents and friends. If these should happen to be filled, latecomers would be seated on the row of benches in front of the desks used by the students as their classes were called up.

My parents and two sisters who were not yet in school found seats at the rear.

Miss Wilson was on the point of beginning the program when a man and a woman accompanied by a girl came up the aisle near where I sat and took seats on a front bench. They had passed before I could see their faces, but I saw that the girl, who appeared to be about my own age, had yellow hair worn in braids down her back. She wore a pink dress.

After a neat little address of welcome by Miss Wilson, the program began. First came the younger pupils with their "pieces," songs, and a little play, then on to the older classes.

I awaited my turn with clammy palms and mental misery which were always present when I was to appear before groups, young as well as older. When my name was called, I dragged my feet to the stage, the teacher's platform that stood six inches above the main floor; licking my lips, I began. I resolutely avoided the tendency, developed from my bashfulness, to look at the floor when speaking and gazed at a spot above the front door.

I got along pretty well until about half through, when I felt a growing awareness of the splash of pink on the front bench which I knew was the dress of the girl with yellow hair. I tried not to let it, but my gaze came down.

I saw the face of a pretty girl, with eyes that looked blue in the light of the hanging kerosene lamps. She was looking at me with a half smile on her lips, with an intentness that indicated she was very much interested in my recitation.

The tingling shock which ran through me stopped my speech cold. Miss Wilson had to prompt me twice before I looked away from the girl and finished my piece. I almost ran back to my seat. What in the world was the matter with me, I thought. I had practiced that piece until I could almost say it backwards.

After my default the program went smoothly enough. Then came Bessie Owens with the final number, announced as a "tragic" drama. Bessie and Miss Wilson had spent a lot of recess and lunch-hour time with that tragedy, every emotion depicted in rolling tones, varied to the situation. Each emotion had its own fluent gestures.

Bessie's melodious voice rose and fell and even sobbed as she told of a gallant girl's struggles with the villainous usurer who was on the point of taking from her invalid father his home and ranch. Then came a struggle between the girl and the villain. With motions and voice depicting loathing, anger, and fierce resolution, Bessie danced about the stage, finally engaging in physical struggle. The villain struck her.

At this point the tragedienne was close to the front edge of the stage, her back to the audience. As the blow was struck, "She staggered back . . ." elocuted Bessie, her tragic tones accompanied by a gesture that brought her hand to her forehead. She did stagger eloquently back—off the platform, to lose balance and fall to the floor flat on her back amid a display of disarranged skirts, petticoats, and ruffles. Men and boys leaped to their feet, eager to lend her aid. But they were given sudden pause when they heard Bessie's clear voice rising from the floor.

". . . and fell to the floor. For a few moments she lay there in a daze,

but . . ." She started to rise. "quickly recovered and regained her feet
. . ." She arose gracefully. ". . . and returned to do battle to the evil
shylock who would steal her father's home. She seized her father's
cane and . . ."

Bessie triumphed, of course. She had the shylock begging for mercy
in no time at all and promising all sorts of things.

The girl's quick wit in an embarrassing situation drew high praise
and rousing applause. I was happy for Bessie, partly because I hoped
that in the excitement of her fine performance the audience might
have forgotten my own ignominious recitation.

Max hadn't forgotten it though. He made a point of stopping at my
desk and saying in a high thin voice:

"Kitty get your tongue?"

With a sneering giggle he went on, and I rejoined my parents. They
were at the door. Father had been talking to the man and woman who
had brought the yellow-haired girl. It was with surprise and some
trepidation that I found Father introducing me to Mr. and Mrs. Wellborn and their daughter, Susan. My handshakes were timid, especially
with the girl, who evidently sensed my embarrassment and tried to
soothe it.

"That was a nice poem you recited," she said, to my surprise.

"I . . . I . . . messed it up," I stuttered.

Susan shrugged. "Oh, we all do that," she said. "You ought to have
heard some of my recitations."

She was smiling and I saw the color of her eyes now. Not just blue,
but lupine blue—deep, verging on purple.

I stuttered something which I hoped she would interpret as thanks
for her kind words. Then she said something that made my heart start
jumping even more than it already was.

"I'm coming to this school after Christmas," she said. "What grade
are you in?"

"Fifth reader," I said.

"Why, so am I! We'll be in the same classes!"

I think I may have said enough halting words to make it clear that
I was very, very glad.

It was thus that an acquaintance began that was to make the following year the happiest I had yet known.

It was well that I could not foretell the future.

CHAPTER 18

The Reef of Norman's Woe

I DON'T BELIEVE MY FATHER AND MOTHER WERE MUCH surprised that I looked forward eagerly to the second half of the school year. They had been young themselves and knew well enough that adolescent crushes were a common thing. It could not be that I had developed a sudden craving for learning to which I had previously shown such indifference.

Susan Wellborn quickly became popular among the students at West End School. She met troubles with a smile, and was ready to help anyone who might need help. She was willing to stay in during recess time to study with those who found the going difficult.

Susan and I were about equal in spelling and reading ability. Once a week Miss Wilson lined up our class and gave us an opportunity to test our spelling skills against each other. She allowed us no room for complacency, giving us more and more difficult words to spell. Susan often spelled me down. I felt glad and let her know it. If I won, she would whisper, "Good for you."

Max was an indifferent reader and speller and it was clear that he was disgruntled by the fact that Susan and I topped him. And, as usual, he never missed an opportunity for a taunt or a mean trick.

So the spring term passed. It was a busy summer for me. I had become big and strong enough to do some real work, and I helped with the potato and hay harvests and with the cattle herd. When the fall school term began, I was happy to find that Susan had been assigned a seat directly across the aisle from mine. But I was not happy to discover that Max was to sit just behind Susan. During the previous term he had tried hard to make up to Susan, but while she was always pleasant to him as she was to everyone, she spent little time with him.

Now that he sat so close, Max had opportunity to work his tricks on me during school hours. He had a little bamboo tube which he used as a blow gun to project spit balls. I got some of these in the neck and face. One morning when I got to school ahead of him I took the tube out of his desk, and crushed it with my heel, then left the pieces on his desk. Then he began throwing the spit balls by hand, but the teacher caught him at it.

Once, as I was leaving the room, Max stuck out his leg and I tripped over it. He wouldn't try that but once, I grimly determined. The next time I had to leave the room during a session I made ready. I was wearing a sturdy pair of shoes with good weight. Rising from my seat, I saw Max turn a little in his. I moved back a little, then took a long step forward with my left foot, and when Max's leg came out, with my right leg I swung a powerful kick at Max's ankle.

The howl Max let out could have been heard a hundred feet away. Of course, Max and I had to stay after school. I noticed Max was limping. He told how I had kicked him without cause. I told just what happened.

The teacher scolded Max, saying she knew he had tripped other pupils. She scolded me for kicking Max instead of reporting the incident to her. She would, she said, notify our parents if there was more trouble between us.

Max limped for a week after that, for which I wasn't sorry. After that he increased his opportunities, when outside, to direct sneering taunts at me. I began to think of physical encounter. I didn't look forward to it. I wasn't very brave, and my isolated life and limited contact with other boys had added to a natural timidity. Yet, if Max continued his dirty works, there would soon be an explosion. This might have been avoided had he not made Susan the victim of one of his tricks.

A crisis was conceived while Max was still limping. During a study hour one afternoon, I became aware of a movement at Max's desk.

Susan was busy working out a problem on her slate when Max moved a hand cautiously over the front of his desk and took hold of one of Susan's braids. He drew it slowly across the top of his desk, pushed aside the sliding top of his ink well, and began to dip the end of her braid, with its bow of ribbon, into the ink. This was at the top of dirty tricks. Revolted and furious, I yelled, "Stop that!"

I was too late. Into the black liquid went the braid and a part of the ribbon. As Susan jerked her head around, she felt the tug of her braid, torn from Max's hand. She drew it over her shoulder, unwittingly smearing ink upon her dress.

The teacher came charging down the aisle, demanding, "Who did that shouting?"

"He did," Max answered, pointing at me. The teacher glared at me and was about to open up at me when Susan's clear voice rang out.

"Herbert was just trying to keep Max from doing this to me!" She held out the braid, and pointed to her stained dress, and then her hand.

The teacher's glare went to Max.

"It just happened to fall in," Max muttered.

"You three stay after school!" she ordered. "Susan, I'll excuse you while you clean up."

The after-school session was brief. Susan told what happened. She was dismissed, as was I with a caution not to disturb classes by shouting. As we left I heard the teacher tell Max that it was the duty of boys to protect girls, and that he hadn't been a gentleman.

I was glad to find next morning that Max had been made to trade seats with another boy who had held the last seat in the row. As I passed him, Max muttered, "Damn liar!"

I was furious, but passed by. There was no sense to the accusation, for Max knew that I knew he was the liar, not I. I was so mad I had visions of knocking his crooked teeth out and smashing his too-big nose.

The chance to try that was very near.

It was the practice of the boys to eat their lunches in the roadway across the ditch where the long cottonwood poles that formed the hitch-racks were strung out and tied between posts. The boys would sit upon or straddle the poles while eating, then flee to their games. This group included the advanced students, among them Joe Kimber.

Joe was a tall, good-looking young man, friendly and ever ready to help others with their studies should help be needed. Not in a regular class, he was learning subjects on the high school level. He helped his brother Walter run their widowed mother's ranch.

I had just finished my lunch when Max, who had been sitting on the next pole, also stood up. I listened to him declaring in a loud voice so I would be sure to hear, that he was now marble champion of the West End, and that I was afraid to play him. I was strung pretty high, but began to leave; that's when Max started to taunt. Upon his face was the sneering grin that had become his trademark. He began to sing out in a high voice:

"Herbie loves Susie! Susie loves Herbie! Herbie's a tattler! Susie's a tattler! Herbie tells lies! Susie tells lies . . ."

Max didn't get any farther than that. I had heard of red rage, and didn't know just what it meant. After that day, I thought I knew; what had been a blue sky turned the color of a sunset. Perhaps I could have restrained myself even then if Max hadn't brought Susan's name into his accusations, but when I heard that lying taunt, the explosion came and I charged.

Max was heavier than I by about fifteen pounds and a little taller, as well as a year older. I didn't think of that now. I didn't know anything about fist fighting, either, but with arms flailing wildly, I tore into Susan's defamer.

Max was taken by surprise, and I got in some good licks before he recovered his wits. Though he had thrown up his arms, I broke through that guard and got a fist into his face and was glad to see the blood begin to run from his nose.

After backing up for a few feet, the advantage I had gained by surprise vanished, and he came at me with his fists. He slugged me in the chest. I answered with a blow to his belly that made him grunt. Then he got a fist in my face. I grabbed at his arms, got a hold, and we fell to the ground.

The school children didn't get a free show like this very often. No sooner had I made my charge when the cry "Fight! Fight!" went up and the boys all left their marbles and baseball and came running. Some of the girls came, too, but one of them ran to tell the teacher and she came charging down the path and across the bridge, fire in her eye.

It was at that point that Joe Kimber took a hand. When Max and I fell to the ground I was on top, but Max turned me over and he was on top when Joe took him by the collar and yanked him to his feet. I scrambled up and was going after Max again when Joe pushed me away, the teacher crying, "Stop! Stop!" and then, "What's the meaning of this?"

"He jumped on me!" Max screamed. "He hit me first!"

Joe Kimber spoke up. He had spent a good deal of time at the dictionary during his school days, had studied composition, and had developed what was called by those he associated with a "polished" type of speech.

"Permit me to put in a word," he said. "I have been a witness to this altercation from its beginning. It was started by Max taunting Herbert and claiming that both he and Susan tattled and lied."

"You're a liar!" shouted Max.

Joe advanced on Max, who started to run, but Joe grabbed him by the collar and the seat of his pants and tossed him into the ditch, which was running full. He turned to the teacher.

"I hope you will not hold it against me that I have taken this means to defend my honor," he said. "Physical force is the only form of retribution this type of miscreant understands. No one shall falsely call me a liar and escape reprisal. I told the truth, and in my opinion Herbert was completely justified in taking action as he did."

The teacher, appearing flabbergasted at Joe's words, stood speechless for a few moments. Then, as Max emerged, sputtering, swearing, and dripping water, she ordered him to go home and change to dry clothes.

When we took our seats at one o'clock, Susan looked at me with concern. My eye had swelled.

"I heard what happened," she said softly. "Thank you for standing up for me, too." She smiled, followed by a little giggle. "Your eye will look pretty, with all those colors around it," she said.

Max returned late in the afternoon. The teacher told him, Joe, and me to stay after school. She then asked Joe to tell exactly what had happened, and he told word for word Max's taunts and described my reaction. She asked for my verification, and I said Joe had told it just right. Then she bent her gaze on Max.

"You have been a disturbing element in this school all year," she told him. "This is to warn you that if you create any more trouble I shall ask the school board to expel you."

Though Max still glowered at me and Susan, and once muttered that next time he would mash my face in, we had no more confrontations.

The rest of the year went smoothly enough. At the "show-off" session on the final day of the fall term, my father and mother were there. Lawrence and Fay were in a patriotic playlet, and of course did fine. Susan and I were teamed up in a short comedy sketch; the scene was a school room, Susan the teacher, and I the scholar. We got through it and I needed only two or three promptings from Susan, which she cleverly turned into a part of the play. Even my parents didn't seem to be aware of the alteration in the script.

An exciting event was to occur during the holidays. We were to have a magic lantern show at the school house the week before Christmas. Our expectations were raised to a high pitch by the wording of the posters that blazed out on cottonwood trees along the roads.

"High in educational value," we were told, which was the key to the school board's permission to use the school house. "Beautiful views in color of the world's wonders. Illustrated recitations of dramatic, heartrending events!"

Father took us all. Speaking for myself, high hopes were satisfied. The school house was jammed full of men, women, boys, and girls, with a number of infants. Kerosene fumes filled the air from the large lamps in the projector. Behind the lights were reflectors that sent the light of the flames through the lenses and onto the screen, a sheet fastened over the blackboards behind the teacher's desk.

The pictures were on glass slides, many of them photographs of natural or hand-drawn scenes, all hand colored. The operator-narrator had a rich, full voice, which he used to express various emotions. After the travel pictures and some comic recitations and views, he went to drama and tragedy. The defiance of Barbara Frietsche was shown, then "The Curfew Shall Not Ring Tonight." Finally came the heartrending recital and views of "The Wreck of the Hesperus."

With the voice of the narrator rising, the recital of the poem accompanied scenes of the good ship under full sail, the approach of the storm, the wave-tossed vessel, the captain's daughter being tied to the mast. When the agonized voice reached out, "And the father answered never a word, for a frozen corpse was he," the tears began to flow. Finally came the smashing of the ship on the reef of Norman's Woe, and the final heartbreaking scene of the beautiful girl still tied to the broken mast, asleep in death, her yellow hair floating around her head.

I heard, through my own tears, the sobs of others. My emotion was accentuated by a tearing thought: the captain's daughter looked so very much like Susan. What if she were lost, too? As we were about to leave the building, I saw Susan with her parents just ahead of us.

157

She smiled and raised her hand. Lanterns hung on either side of the entrance, and as Susan moved away, they cast a yellow light on her head with strange effect. Her hair wasn't just yellow anymore. The light gave her braids the color and texture of woven threads of pure spun gold.

We had a pleasant Christmas that year. The potato crop had been good. Father had marketed a nice lot of fat beef. There was enough hay in stock to ensure a good winter feeding for his cattle. There was money in the bank.

"We'll start our new house this year," I heard Father tell Mother. "You have gone too long with too little. I'll get a man to help Lyssie with the cattle, and Chappo knows how to make good 'dobe bricks."

We would have water piped into the house. There would be a big solar heater. We'd have a water tank on a tower and a windmill to pump water for it. Later would come a good barn and another windmill for the stock. He didn't trust ditch water any more.

When I asked Father if there would be enough wind for two windmills, he laughed, and said, "You've been reading the Farmers' Almanac."

I thought a lot about Susan. One night I had a dream, a bad dream, that brought me awake, crying out. I saw the scene where the captain's daughter floated with the broken mast, but now it wasn't the captain's daughter. It was Susan. I had trouble getting back to sleep, and was left with a feeling of foreboding.

I was glad when that January Monday came; I saddled my horse and rode to school. I unsaddled and crossed the plank bridge and started down the path to the school. A group of boys was gathered there. They looked toward me as one said,

"Well, I hear our little Susie is no more."

"Yes," said another. "She died of inflammation of the bowels. Too much candy and nuts."

I can hear those words today as clearly as I heard them then. I didn't stop to ask questions, but walked blindly on, through the door and to my desk.

When school had taken up, the teacher rapped for order. She spoke of Susan's untimely death, and paid tribute to her fine personality, her friendliness to all, her help to those who needed it, and her fine scholarship and qualities in general.

The best medical talent available had been called to her aid, but to no avail. If only medical science had been more advanced then! I don't suppose anyone in the school would have recognized the words "acute appendicitis."

I was still in a daze when the reading class was called up. I reached in my desk for my reader, and when I drew it out I saw something protruding from under the front cover.

It was a Christmas card. Not a cheap one such as could be bought for a few pennies, but one designed and painted by hand in water colors. There was a pretty little Christmas scene, and a message. It read:

"Merry Christmas, Herbert, and a Happy New Year. Susan."

I knew tears were coming that I could no longer hold back. With the card in my hand I jumped up, ran to the door and through it, and out across the ditch. I paid no heed to the voice of the teacher calling for me to come back. Putting the card in a pocket, I hurriedly went to my horse. For a few moments I stood with my face against the horse's neck, trying very hard to choke back the sobs, finally succeeding. Big boys shouldn't cry. Not ones big enough to rope and tie a calf.

I began to saddle up. Lawrence came out.

"Teacher says to come back," he said.

"I'm going home," I said. I cinched up, climbed into the saddle and rode away.

It was a cloudy day. Rain seemed near. The ride home was lonely and bleak. Frost and wind had stripped the trees of leaves. Tumble-weeds along the road had curled themselves into balls, ready to go rolling away to seek new places to drop their seeds.

Mother hurried to the corral when I rode up. Looking at my face, she cried out:

"Are you sick?"

"Susan is dead," I told her.

We went to the house. I showed her Susan's card.

"Sweet," she said. She gave me then the comfort that only mothers can give.

For a long time I treasured Susan's Christmas card. Somewhere along the way it was lost, but I wish I had it still as a warm expression of sympathy and friendship from a bright and happy spirit who had done so much to smooth a rough path for a lonely, bashful boy.

CHAPTER 19

Lead, Kindly Light

1897

AFTER THE CHRISTMAS HOLIDAYS, SCHOOL WAS JUST SOME-
thing to be endured. With February, trees began to bud and grass and
filaree began to grow. Then blue skies, warm winds, sun, and flowers
transformed the desert again into carpets of glowing beauty.

We also had a growing interest now. This was the year that we
were to begin our new house.

"We'll start building when the potato crop is harvested," Father
said. "Meantime we'll be getting ready."

On a Saturday he asked me to come with him. Carrying a bundle
of stakes, a hammer, a long measuring tape, a compass and square, he
led me to the site of the new home. That morning we staked out the
homesite and lined out the trenches for the foundation. It was exciting
to see how large the house would be, with eight rooms now planned
and screened sleeping rooms besides.

It had been a long time since Father and Mother had been so cheerful. The little two-room shack could be turned into a storage house at
last.

It was in May, near the end of the school year, when Father did not
arise from his bed one morning. He had been driving himself hard, and

was thinner than he should have been. He now had a fever, and Mother knew he must be very ill indeed. Nothing else would have kept him from his work.

"We must get you to a doctor," Mother told him. Over his protest she called Lyssie and told him he must drive them to town. Lyssie was soon ready with the best trotter Father owned hitched to the buggy. Father, seated between Mother and Lyssie, was driven swiftly away. Fay and I did not go to school. She stayed to look after Virna and Vivian, and Lawrence joined Chappo in tending the cattle.

Lyssie returned alone that evening with bad news.

"Dr. Battin says your father has typhoid fever," he told us. "He put him in an isolated room in a little two-story hotel, and your mother will stay with him as nurse.

"She's pretty badly worried about you children." He twisted his moustache. "Especially you girls." He was really worried, with five children on his hands, the oldest not yet fifteen.

"Mrs. Lockwood once asked us to visit them," Fay said.

Lyssie grasped at that, and next morning rode to the Lockwood ranch and told that fine lady of his problem. That same afternoon she arrived with Alfred in their surrey, helped the three girls pack the necessary clothes, and took them to her home. Before she left, she helped Lyssie get together some clothes and toilet articles Mother had asked him to bring her.

The next day Lyssie took me with him to Phoenix. There I went up the first stairs I had ever climbed. Mother answered Lyssie's knock, and I was shocked at how pale and tired she looked. But she smiled and said, "I'm so glad you could come, Herbert. But I can't hug and kiss you—you must not get too close to either Papa or me. Typhoid is very contagious."

She was very much relieved when I told her Mrs. Lockwood had taken the girls. Then, "Papa, Herbert is here."

I moved as close to the bed on which my father lay as I dared. I was really frightened to see how very pale and thin he appeared.

"Hello, Papa," I said.

Father tried to raise his head, but managed only to turn it a little.

"How are you son? I'm . . . so glad . . . you could come. How are Lawrence and . . . the girls?"

I told him how things were at the ranch. He didn't say anything. He seemed to be sleeping. Then he aroused and said "Mama," and I went out and sat on the stairs. I waited a long time. Lyssie came back.

Then Mother opened the door and asked me to come back in. Lyssie told her he was ready to go. She told him to go in and speak to Father. He came out looking greatly worried.

"Now tell your Papa goodbye," she said.

I went back into the gloomy, starkly furnished room. Father seemed to be asleep.

"I'm going now, Papa," I said. It was hard for me to speak. Father didn't answer. I moved closer and spoke louder.

"Goodbye, Papa."

He opened his eyes, and answered in a voice I had to strain to hear.

"Goodbye, son. When I get home . . . we'll start . . . the new house." A pause, then came words that burned themselves into my brain. They were spoken almost in a whisper.

"God bless you, my boy."

Choking, I left the room, gasping out a goodbye to Mother. My eyes were so blinded by tears that Lyssie had to help me down the stairs. Not a word was uttered on the drive home.

I managed to convey to Lawrence how very ill Father seemed to be, and my dread of what the consequences of that illness might be. Never before had our parents been away from us for more than a day at a time. Their absence now gave us an understanding of how much we had relied on their strength of mind and hand, and how terrible it would be if either of those towers of strength should fall. Lyssie tried to give us some words of comfort, but was unconvincing.

The next day, I joined Lyssie and Lawrence in riding herd. They had remained unattended for a few days while other ranch duties demanded attention; the cattle took advantage of the opportunity and had begun to scatter. Chappo remained on the ranch to handle irrigation and the care of the penned livestock.

The third day was Sunday, and though work with stock and fields had to go on, everyone knocked off early. Shortly after we reached the house, we saw a horse and buggy coming down the lane and on to the house.

It was Mrs. Lockwood. She called Lyssie aside and talked with him for several minutes. Then she drove away without talking to Lawrence and me.

Lyssie was sitting on a chair under the shade at the front of the house as we approached him, anxious to learn what message our visitor had borne. He was staring at the ground. Nervously, almost violently, he was pulling at his moustache, twisting the ends first with one hand, then the other. Finally, he raised his head and looked at us. Twice he opened his mouth to speak, but words failed him. Then they came out.

"Well, did you know your father is dead?"

Though I had feared that dreadful message might come, the words struck with the force of a blow. Both Lawrence and I stood speechless, rooted in our places. Lawrence recovered first enough to utter one word, his inflection indicating wonderment and disbelief.

"Dead?"

Then he turned away. I sought shelter in the mesquite grove, where I could be alone until I had weathered the first blasts of this storm of grief.

Mrs. Battin took Mother in charge, while Mrs. Lockwood and her daughters helped prepare Fay, Virna, and Vivian for the funeral held two days later.

Viewing Father for the last time before the lid to the coffin was closed was a terrible experience for us all. He looked so peaceful lying there, younger than in life. He wasn't actually very old. There were so many things he had wanted to do.

The funeral was held in the First Methodist Church at Phoenix, and "Lead, Kindly Light" was beautifully sung by a member of the choir.

The Lockwoods and the Battins saw us safely home. The absence of father and husband in a house over which a pall of loneliness had fallen brought a feeling of deeper grief to mother and children. No more would we hear Father's cheerful greeting as he came in from field or range or from a trip to town, nor feel his comforting arms around us. With Mother, he had given each of us children an equal share of affection, with never a hint of favoritism. His plans for the future were ended. The new house, for which both he and Mother had given up so much, would never be built.

After supper Mother gathered us together. She explained to us how our father's death had created new problems that we must meet with courage. She asked us to help her make plans.

"The time for crying is over," she said. But it was not quite over. She led us in bedtime devotion. We recited the twenty-third psalm and prayed to God for guidance in life's future. But when she tried to lead us in singing "Lead, Kindly Light," she broke down and wept.

"I feel that half of me is gone," she told us afterward. "Now you children will have to make up the other half."

The next day, after talking it over with her flock, she called in Lyssie.

"I've been thinking a lonely ranch may not be the place for a widow to raise her children," she said. "I have their education to think of. If we decide to leave, will you run the ranch on shares?"

Lyssie agreed to this.

"Meantime," Mother said, "please take charge of the potato and hay harvesting."

The Lockwoods visited us frequently and sometimes Alfred would drive out alone to see how we were getting on. Learning of my fascinating for adventure stories, he brought me a copy of *Lorna Doone*.

"I think this is one of the finest stories of adventure and romance ever written," he told me.

The adventures of John Ridd and his precarious romance with Lorna Doone thrilled me to the core. He brought other books and they helped us all to forget our loneliness, if only briefly.

Mother's own father had died the year before, and now her mother wrote asking her to return to Ohio and stay with her. Mother's two younger sisters would be attending college. A good school was within walking distance of our grandmother's farm home. So, with the agreement of her children, she decided to go back to the home that had been hers before her marriage.

To raise money and to make it easier for Lyssie, she made arrangements to sell the better part of her herd of cattle. Alfred arranged for Charles T. Hirst, a Phoenix real estate and cattle broker, to call on Mother. He did so, bringing his wife and two children, Helen and Lewis, to visit with us. Thus we gained more fine and enduring friendships. Many kindnesses were shown us by people in the West End and in Phoenix, some of whom we had known only slightly or not at all.

Phoenix now had two rail terminals. The dusty stage line from Maricopa on the Southern Pacific that my father had ridden had been replaced by a branch rail line; from the north, a rail was laid from Ash Fork on the Atchison, Topeka and Santa Fe road. It was this route we chose for the trip to Ohio.

As Mother packed her trunks, there were tears in her eyes she could not hold back as she carefully tucked away the pack of letters she had received from Father during their separation. She never parted with those.

Then Lyssie drove us to Phoenix for the last time in the Studebaker

164

wagon, its green and orange paint fading and peeling. We had our last look at that part of the desert we knew so well. Soon we were among the mountains and the first pines we had ever seen. We were on the way to new cities, new schools.

But the West was in Mother's blood. After four years in Ohio, she moved with her five children to Los Angeles in 1902; California was to be our home for less than two years. In mid-1903, Lyssie informed Mother he wished to leave the Arizona ranch, and suggested that as Lawrence was then nineteen years old he should be able to take over the operation of the ranch and the cattle herd. Lawrence was glad to accept the challenge, and returned to the old homestead. I joined him there at the beginning of 1904. Mother and the girls followed later in the year and established a home in Phoenix.

Two years later, Mother sold the ranch and bought a tract only a mile from the center of Phoenix. There, the plans she and Father had made for a comfortable home came to fruition. In 1910, this was exchanged for a fine fruit ranch in central Arizona, on the Verde River near the mining town of Jerome. The following year, Mother bought a residence in Phoenix for herself and the girls, and I joined Lawrence at the Verde River ranch.

I quit ranching in 1912 for a position in the administration department of the United Verde Copper Company mine and smelter at Jerome and Clarkdale, where I remained until retirement.

Though away from the hard work she and my father experienced during their years on the ranch, my mother always looked back with pleasure on those years at "Brushwood Manor." She loved the desert, and took up her brushes again to paint scenes she held in memory. When spring would come for its annual visit, Mother would say, "Let's go out and see the desert flowers." So we would take her out to where mesquite, palo verde, sage, and cactus grew—where the open spaces between the higher growth were carpeted with gorgeous flowers such as only the desert can display so well.

Mother would gaze long and silently; at times, we could see tears in her eyes. We knew then that she was thinking of the golden days, when she stood with the man she loved, their arms entwined—gazing at just such scenes, inhaling the desert scents, and feeling the warm winds and the sun.

Epilogue

The Young Family

FRANCIS ASBURY YOUNG, born in Ohio in 1851. Filed on a homestead in Arizona in 1886, where his wife and two children joined him in same year. He died in 1897 at age 46.

EVA NAOMI LAWRENCE YOUNG, born in Ohio in 1859. She died in Phoenix in 1923 at age 64.

LAWRENCE LEROY YOUNG, born in Ohio in 1884. After retiring from ranching he engaged in land development and building. He died in Phoenix in 1980 at age 95.

ELVA FAY YOUNG MACDONALD, born in Ohio in 1885. She established her own business in Phoenix, dealing in real estate, insurance, and other enterprises. She died in Phoenix in 1966 at age 81.

HERBERT VERNON YOUNG, born on his father's homestead in 1887. After a business college course, he engaged in secretarial work. In 1912 he became secretary to the General Manager of the United Verde Copper Company at Jerome and Clarkdale, remaining with this firm for 41 years. He lives at Clarkdale, where he pursues his avocation of writing.

VIRNA MAY YOUNG, born at her father's ranch in 1890. She graduated from Tempe Normal School, now Arizona State University, taught school in Clarkdale and Phoenix. She studied nursing and entered the service of St. Luke's Hospital in San Francisco, where she remained as Instructor of Nurses until her retirement. Her home is in Clarkdale.

VIVIAN FLORINE YOUNG, born 1892 on the family ranch. After high school she studied at Columbia School of Dramatics in Chicago and performed on a chatauqua circuit. She then became an instructor of dramatics and dancing at the Arizona School of Music. Following the death of her husband, in later years she served as secretary to the Arizona State Highway Commission until her retirement. She died in 1980 at age 88.

ULYSSES ("LYSSIE") GRANT YOUNG, a second cousin of Francis Young, born c. 1865 in Kansas. He immigrated to Arizona in 1889, soon after Francis Young established his homestead. He traveled, but spent most of his years on this ranch before Francis Young's death, and six years afterward. He helped Lawrence on the Verde fruit ranch and farmed his own ranch near Phoenix until his death in c. 1948 at age 83.